The Meaning of the Goetheanum Windows

Rudolf Steiner's story of the Spiritual Quest carved into nine stained glass windows

Adrian Anderson Ph.D.

Threshold Publishing, 2016
www.rudolfsteinerstudies.com

Distributed by Dennis Jones P/L - Port Campbell Press
Bayswater VIC
Australia

ISBN 978-0-9941602-3-2 (pbk)
ISBN 978-0-9941602-4-9 (hbk)

Contents

Illustrations

Foreword

In the village of Dornach, near Basel in Switzerland, is located the impressive building which, under the auspices of the Anthroposophical Society, serves as the Centre for conferences and training courses based on the work of Rudolf Steiner (1861-1925). The Goetheanum is a striking sight; a huge building designed in an organic architectural style, and one of the first buildings in the world to be constructed out of reinforced concrete. The current building, the 'second Goetheanum', was constructed during the 1920's, after the first Goetheanum, made of wood, was burnt down at the end of 1922.

Looking at it from the outside, the visitor can see nine huge windows set into its walls. They have a soft white appearance, because each window has an outer pane of milky-coloured glass placed over it, to give the right tone to the colour of the stained-glass windows, when they are seen from inside the building. Once you're inside, you can see that intriguing scenes have been carved into the glass. A very impressive feature of these windows is that the scenes in them have been actually carved into the glass. Rudolf Steiner especially directed the artist to use a scratching technique when carving the scenes, rather than just making the usual straight lines. This gives a marvellous, living quality to the imagery.

I hope that this book will help both the tourist, as well as those who have prior knowledge of Rudolf Steiner's teachings, to appreciate the meaning of these windows. My understanding of these scenes is based on the brief written and verbal indications by Rudolf Steiner; these have guided me in my decades of contemplating them. We shall go on a fascinating and inspiring journey together as we contemplate each of these windows ! These scenes, carved into the glass panels, depict key elements of the pathway to spiritual development, which could be called a self-initiation process.

The images used for this book
The technique of carving glass was invented by Rudolf Steiner about 1915. He also designed a tool with which the glass could be cut into, or carved, by the various artists undertaking this task. The windows of the second Goetheanum were carved by a Russian artist, Assia Turgenieff. The images of the windows used in this book are enhanced versions of the coloured drawings used to carve these scenes into the glass. These drawings were made by this artist, from the sketches provided to her by Rudolf Steiner. I have chosen these drawings because it is easier to see some details in them than in the actual glass windows. This is especially true of the last two windows; they are of the wrong colour, and consequently their engravings are every difficult to see.

After the fire which destroyed the first building, new windows were cast in a glass-works factory, but unfortunately, in the process of casting these huge panes, the last two windows, the ones nearer to the stage, or eastern end of the building, which were meant to be pink in colour, came out in a bright orange colour (the blue component of the dye substances had not been absorbed).

The drawings used here have also been chosen because they present the colour, shape and architectural setting of the panes of glass, specified by Rudolf Steiner for the first building, which was a different style to the current Goetheanum (see below for more about this). So my intention is to help the reader to be able to contemplate these huge and fascinating windows as they were originally intended to be experienced, by a person walking through the first Goetheanum.

If you are a visitor to the Goetheanum and have not read any of Rudolf Steiner's works, this book will provide you with a useful and informed explanation of the windows. If then you would like to get to know more about Rudolf Steiner, then one of my books, the *Rudolf Steiner Handbook*, offers a clear and comprehensive presentation of his world-view, called 'anthroposophy', it has many pages of coloured diagrams and other images that help the reader to grasp his message.

If you have a background in Rudolf Steiner's teachings, then **Part Two** of the commentary for each window will take you deeper into the meaning of these scenes.

1 Top: the first Goetheanum with its whitish windows visible as 3 sets of curved panels, in a wooden framework on the south side; they have a broad, more horizontal form.
Below: the second Goetheanum; to the left side is the front, where the red window with its two upright supporting beams is visible above the trees; and along the south side, the four windows can be seen (one is obscured); they are narrow and vertical in their shape.

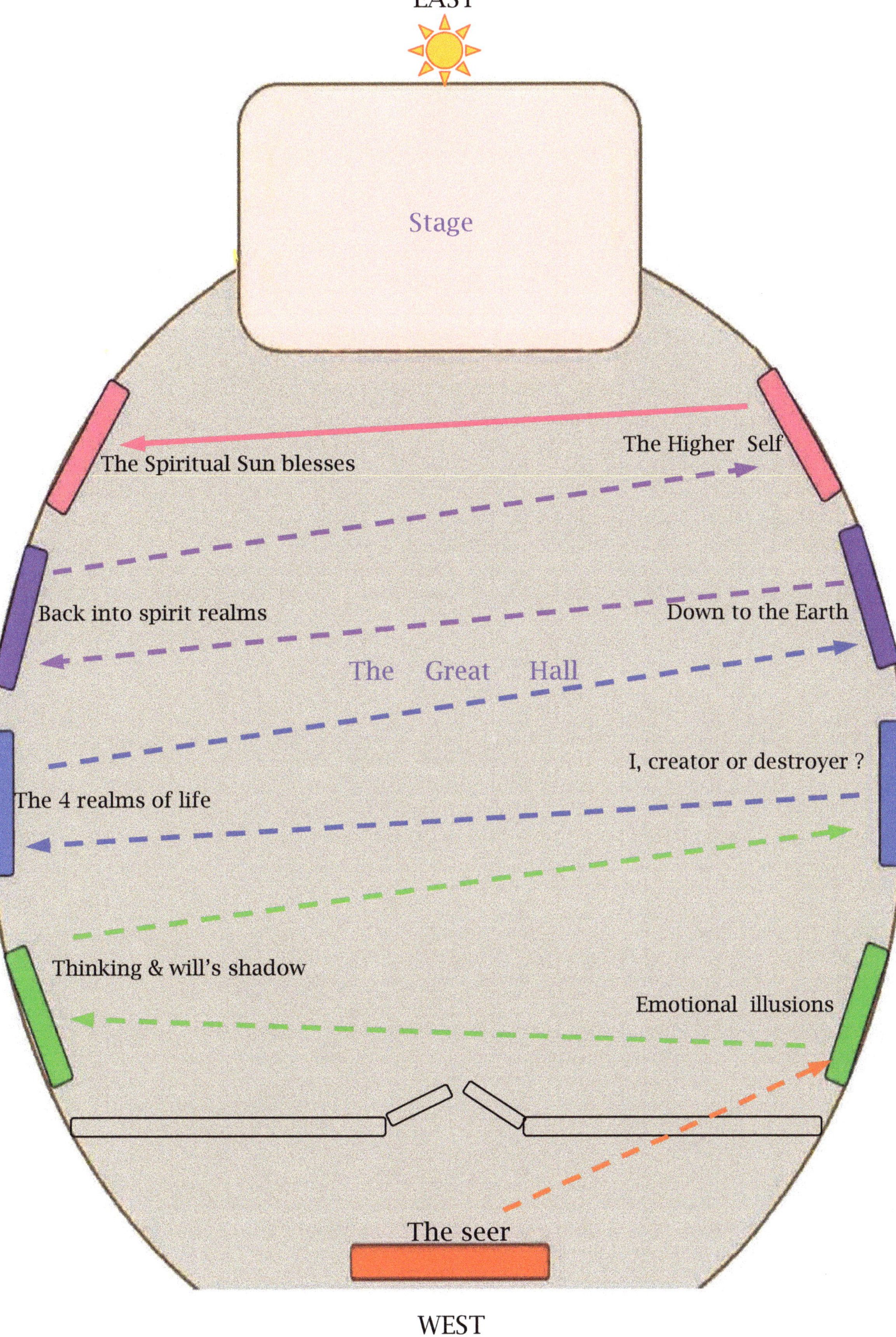

2 The position of the 9 windows in the Goetheanum, based on the first building

Introduction

Background

In the current Goetheanum, the windows are thin and tall, so they have a 'vertical axis' one could say; but in the first building the windows were broader and not so high, so they had a 'horizontal axis', and also they were beautifully arched in their upper part, as Illustration 1 shows. The different shaping used for the second Goetheanum was necessary as this building itself is much taller than the first Goetheanum.

All of these windows have three parts, so technically they are each a 'triptych': that is, artwork with three sections. This threefold design allows each window to show firstly, the given situation of a person seeking spiritual development, then in the middle pane, the main achievement or lesson to be learnt, and in the right pane, the outcome of this process, or the way to getting this desired outcome. The windows also have four features: their colour, shape, a meditative script and of course, their extraordinary scenes. (The script is not used in the building; it not actually placed on, or near, the relevant window.) In the first building, the top of the windows formed three arches, with a large arch in the middle and two smaller arches on either side. The two minor panels were on each side of the larger central panel. In terms of the observer, experiencing similar, rounded architectural forms all around them in the first Goetheanum, this arched quality must have been very agreeable. The architectural form of a work of art speaks perhaps as strongly as its colour. As Turgenieff wrote, "One could see how favourable the first building had been, for {observing} the play of light and colour of the windows...as all the colour radiating in from the windows, met in the centre of the hall."[1] I feel that this earlier shape allows the viewer to grasp the message of the windows more clearly than the current tall, vertical shape. In the new building, what were two side panels are now placed underneath as two scenes, with the central scene placed above these two in a single panel.

So, in the old building, the main scene was in the larger central panel, the left side panel showed the beginning stage of the spiritual situation or challenge, while the small panel on the right, showed the progress being made, or that has been made. For this reason, here the windows are presented in this older, arched form. This is made possible by using copies of the original drawings made by Assia Turgenieff. Since the colour in these century-old drawings has now faded, they have been enhanced by a computer program, and the effort has been made to get near to the intended colours, especially the pink windows.

These drawings are also the best way to appreciate the windows, that is, to see the scenes that belong to each window, as these graphics are sometimes more clearly shown in coloured drawings, than in photos or slides of the actual glass panes; especially with regard to what are today's windows in a bright orange. There are nine windows altogether: one large red one and inside the Great Hall, four sets of two windows, one of the south side and one on the north side. The first set is green in colour, followed by blue, purple and pink sets, one each in the northern and southern sides of the hall, see Illustration 2. In the first Goetheanum, the central panels were 4.2m high, and 1.4m wide; the side panels were 3.7m high, and .72m wide. In the second building the panels are from 6m to 8m high and 2 metres wide; the glass panes themselves are 1.5 cm thick.

Rudolf Steiner's intention in having these nine windows inserted into the walls of the building was to offer insights to the viewer into the spiritual nature of the human being and in particular, into the main dynamics in a person's life if one decides to go on the quest for spiritual development today. The first window, in vibrant red, shows the end result of the quest, the other

---

[1] Assia Turgenieff, memoirs, *Die Goetheanum Fenster-Motive*, 1935, p.32.

The Red Window

Initiation

It has manifested *I am beholding* *It manifests*

four sets of windows, in green, then blue, then purple and finally pink, take the viewer deeper into the link between the human being, who is awakening their higher self, and the spiritual worlds.

THE RED WINDOW

Before we start our explorations of the windows, it is important to note that the themes which underlie the scenes carved into the windows present spiritual teachings, about the process of spiritual development. But in doing this, many themes in anthroposophy in general are incorporated. These are themes which Rudolf Steiner often explained in detail, on the basis of his vast research work, published in some 360 volumes, so far. In this book, it is not intended to comment in detail on these subjects; instead an overview of such subjects will be presented, and information given as to where to read further. My *Rudolf Steiner Handbook* does provide an explanation of most of the themes associated with the windows. Rudolf Steiner's world-view is derived from what he termed 'anthroposophy' which means the wisdom that the spiritualized human being can attain. Also, there are some terms which are used in Rudolf Steiner's teachings that you may not be familiar with; these are briefly explained when they are first used, and there is also a small dictionary (or 'glossary') of such words at the back of the book.

The Goetheanum is so designed, that anyone who walks up the staircase towards the entrance of the Great Hall can see the red window on their left. But only those who actually enter the Hall can see the other eight windows. This design feature already indicates that the red window presents an over-view of the process of spiritual development to the general visitor. But the powerful processes involved in spiritual development are only revealed if you 'cross the threshold' and go into the Great Hall, as illustration 2 shows. So what do we see as we gaze at this huge red window? This window today is still in the horizontal style, just as it was in the first Goetheanum. Let's consider now the keynote words or meditative script, written by Rudolf Steiner about this window, and then its colour and then the themes depicted. There is a kind of keynote script about each panel from Rudolf Steiner, and some of the windows have their own 'over-script', as well.

Colour Overview

Let's contemplate the significance of the colour red for the soul. Red in the aura shows satisfaction in being active, or happiness in a particular moment, and someone who enjoys participating in events in general. It has an outgoing active influence on the soul. And as a special extension of this inner soul quality of red, Rudolf Steiner stated in regard to this colour that it has a living elemental influence, "which provides the most beneficial energies for the future of humanity's existence on the Earth."[2] These mysterious words are indicating that colour is not only an inert thing, it has a kind of subtle life to it; it is a doorway for certain spiritual energies. So the influence on the soul of the powerful, pure red colour is that you want to be active, and your activity wants to contribute to a better future for everyone. And this includes undertaking spiritual development.

Thematic Overview: *Initiation*

Rudolf Steiner wrote above his sketch for the red window this one word, which tells us what the theme of this window is, in general. As we shall see, the central panel refers to the dynamics in a person who has been initiated; that is, who has gained enlightenment to some extent, and who is therefore also a seer: see illustration 3.

A brief overview of the scenes

In the **left** panel: a despondent human being; below are three unpleasant entities.

In the **central** panel: a human countenance; it is impersonal, gazing out at the viewer, and many unusual energies or beings are in the aura of this person.

In the **right** panel: a positive, exulting human being with three sets of divine beings within.

---

[2] GA 284, 15th Oct. 1911.

4 The Three Beasts
These depict (from left to right) the shadow-side of thinking, will and feeling. They have been coloured here for clarity and to aid those familiar with Rudolf Steiner's 1924 meditation lessons.

The left panel of the Red Window

Keynote script: ***Es offenbart* = *It manifests***

Let's focus on the left panel first. A human being is there, and her or his body language is presenting the message that this person is not happy about their life in terms of spiritual development. They are unsure of where they are wanting to go, and how to proceed in relation to this. Below this person, veiled within a dark area, are three ugly entities which we could call 'three beasts'. These three unpleasant figures are more easily seen in the enlargement that I have made of them, see illustration 4, where they have been coloured to help clarify their meaning for those who are familiar with Rudolf Steiner's work.

The script for this panel is echoing this person's body language: someone who is not inwardly alert, and who is puzzled about how to move forwards spiritually. Their personality manifests as given; no especial inner development has been undertaken., The three unpleasant figures or monsters, underneath the person, and somewhat hidden, are qualities in his or her soul which are hidden from their conscious mind.[3] A student of anthroposophy did ask Rudolf Steiner if these three monsters represented the negative qualities of the three strands of our mind, or soul: thinking, will and feeling. He answered, "Just don't have an abstract schematic view; in that way, you block your access to them. These 'monsters' are realities, they are not abstract ideas."[4]

So, they do represent the negative thinking, emotions and will; but one needs to approach them in a living, dynamic way and to realize that these three unpleasant images represent a reality in a powerfully esoteric way. They are those portions of our thinking, feeling and will, in which various self-centred, egoistic, un-spiritual qualities dominate. We can note here that it is a pivotal theme in Rudolf Steiner's teachings, that our consciousness or soul is linked to spiritual realities. The higher soul qualities are linked to the angels, and our lower qualities are subject to influences from negative spirit beings.

More precisely, the anti-social, even malignant, qualities in the lower impulses, are due to the influence of the two classes of negative spiritual beings about which anthroposophical wisdom provides deep insights. Rudolf Steiner calls these the 'Luciferic' and 'Ahrimanic' beings. The 'Luciferic' spirits bring about states of soul, which result in naïve thinking and self-centred desires; whereas the 'Ahrimanic' spirits, bring about a callous, even cruel, will, and also a cold way of thinking, or at best a materialistic way of thinking which denies the spiritual side of life.[5]

On the left is a clumsy, heavy bird. One gets the impression that this bird cannot fly; and its eyes are glassy and empty. This figure graphically presents the kind of thinking which is 'earth-bound', that is, an attitude of mind which is not able to accept spiritual ideas. Such thinking rejects ideas about everything beyond the material world, especially spiritual realms and spirit beings. So this figure is depicting **doubt** in the existence of spiritual realities.

The entity on the right slightly resembles a human being; it has prominent teeth and dead, wiry bits of hair. It is about the lower un-spiritual, unclean desires and emotions. In particular, it depicts the soul-state in which **fear** of spirituality, and of spiritual realms, dominates. This kind of soul-state fears the prospect of high morality, of purity, of a kind, selfless, warm-hearted way of feeling. For all of these imply the end of its self-centred life and indulgence in lowly pleasures. This state of soul makes people express their antipathy to spirituality in a veiled way. They become sarcastic about spirituality; they want to mock it.

But when the emotions are so imprisoned in a lowly ego-centric state, the result is that the intellect becomes too predominant, and the emotions shrivelled up. This person can be very clever, but their emotional life eventually suffers; this could lead to physical illnesses and or mental health problems. The teeth are the most hardened part of the body, and therefore here

---

[3] The interpretation (G. Hartmann) that the person has clambered up the 'rock' is unconvincing, as it appears to contradict the message of the panel, that the person is unaware of their lower-self and its power, hidden inside their soul.

[4] Memoirs of A. Turgenieff, p.14, Dornach, 1935.

[5] These names and the influence of these beings are clearly explained in my *Rudolf Steiner Handbook*, which also offers a guide as to what books to begin with, if you want to know more about Rudolf Steiner's teachings.

they are huge; this presents artistically the inner hardening of the emotional capacities through self-centred, un-enlightened desires and feelings. Likewise the deadened hair represents unwise, un-spiritual consciousness, following anthroposophical understanding that our hair is the result of spiritual energy streams condensing into matter; if the hair becomes so hardened and deadened, then one's consciousness has likewise become deadened.[6]

Finally, in the middle of the three, is the largest and most powerful of the negative soul qualities: evil or anti-social **Will**. In this negative force, there is **hate** of the good, of the spiritual, and thus a lack of social conscience, a lack of interest in the needs of other people. The form of the third beast is a masterly artistic portrayal (or metaphor), of the anti-social will.* What do we see with this beast? We see a hardened being – it is quite bonelike – with almost no limbs; it has four small legs. They remind us not of a human being, but of animals, so this is then 'the Beast' in the human being; a human being who has hatred of the spiritual, of the divine. (Note: when a star * appears, this means that, in **Part Two** of the section on that window, a deeper, more esoteric view of the subject is given. For our will is operative in us through our limbs; here the limbs are tiny, and very significantly, the upper limbs, that is our arms and hands, are absent here.

It is with our hands that our will (or our 'volition' in psychological terms), does so many complex and often fine deeds: whether in nursing, healing, design work, parenting, artistic activity, and so on. The body is seen in anthroposophy as having three features, which serve as the organs of the three-fold human soul: the thinking, using the head, the feelings or emotions, using the heart and lungs. Thirdly, the will, using the limbs, which are empowered by the digestive system which creates and stores up sugars and proteins.

Although this entity is not a person, it does represent a negative human reality; so we can say that it is making a powerful statement about the hidden, shadow-side of the human being, of the will. What is it saying? That in this hidden, unethical will, there is no true will; it has no organs to manifest our normal, decent will. It is an artistic meditation on 'anti-will', or the non-existence of that good will [7] which is at the core of every decent human being.

Also, we have another limb or organ for our will – the jaw and mouth, through which we speak. This power to speak, to create language as a vessel for our thoughts, is in many ways the highest expression of human consciousness or will.* This beast has no mouth; it is unable to speak. It becomes clear now that the script for this left panel of the window, "*it manifests*", tells us that here, the ordinary, un-developed state of human beings, with the veiled lower-self, is being shown.

The right panel of the Red Window

Keynote script: ***Es hat geoffenbart*** = ***It has manifested***

Over on the right panel of the window, we see the opposite of what is on the left side; the person is triumphant, exulting, gazing up to the sun. But in this window, the sun represents what Rudolf Steiner calls the **'spiritual sun'**. This unusual term means the Divine, but in its most powerful manifestation within our solar system. The reason that the divine is depicted as the sun (but not the physical sun disk) is because in the anthroposophical world-view, behind every material thing there exists a spiritual reality. For example, when we see another human being, we really only see their material body; but there is also a life-force, and an aura which is how the soul appears to the clairvoyant. In addition, there is also that person's Spiritual-self, which has its own aura, formed from a much higher kind of spiritual 'substance'. This is what is commonly called 'the human spirit'. How much of that is present in a person depends upon the degree of spiritual development of each individual.

---

[6] GA 117, lects. 22nd Nov. & 7th Dec. 1909.

[7] This is known as 'agape' in early Greek texts from Christianity; it can be called 'spiritual love'.

Likewise, the sun has not only its radiant physical body, and an immense life-force, but also a 'soul' aura and a 'spiritual' aura. On these higher levels, it is a habitation for many divine beings. The planets in our solar system, as well as the Earth with humanity and animal species (or, to use a poetic expression, the various 'life-waves' on Earth), were all created in the first instance by the high spiritual beings who exist on the spiritual aspect of the sun. (There are even higher Powers, and a point of origin of Creation beyond the sun, but that is not the theme of this panel.) It is from clairvoyant awareness of this situation by the priests and priestesses, that in ancient times, the sun – or rather, the divine beings associated with the physical disc – were worshipped. This spiritual sun is depicted in most of the windows, and in the spiritual realms is experienced as a radiant spiritual reality.

That the sun has several layers of being (as do we human beings), was a very prominent and widespread view in ancient cultures. The Emperor, Julian the Apostate (AD 331-363) who was initiated into the Mithraic Mysteries, wrote a treatise expounding on this perception. In this he teaches that 'king Helios' has the power to make visible all things in creation, and this is done by "the visible disk" of Helios. But additionally, the Earth-sphere contains many beings in the state of developing, and it is the second level of the sun he says, that "sustains this developing process... as well as creating the form and being-ness to the solar angels". He also tells his readers that the ancient Phoenician initiates, in regard to Helios, declared that on a higher level, "the untainted light-rays spread out everywhere through creation are the manifestation of pure spirit".[8] This level is the 'Devachanic' or actual spirit realm of creation.

Also many ancient Egyptian hymns to the sun express a similar idea, of the Divine as powerfully manifesting through the sun, and not just physically by day, but also as a radiant sphere "at night", that is, in spiritual realms. For example, such expressions are in Egyptian literature as,

> Hail to thee, Re-*Atum Khepri Harakh-te*, divine soul illumining the nether world with the rays of his bright divine eye, who shines by day {but is also} Lord of the Night.[9]

The long name given here for the sun god 'Re', refers of the sun on a spiritual level, in regard to its many ways of affecting both the physical and spiritual realms.[10] So in the right panel, this triumphant person has attained to seership and high spirituality, and is facing what we normally call 'the divine'. But Rudolf Steiner here is more precisely describing this as the Spiritual-sun. Hence for the meditant in this window, in the right panel, the three 'monsters' have virtually disappeared from her or his soul, and are replaced by three sets of divine beings. These are presumably Angels, bestowing wisdom, purity and goodness in the soul, and creating a much more empowered and ennobled Spiritual-self. So here the script reads, "*it has manifested*", meaning that this person has been successful in manifesting their spiritual potential, and finding their higher-self. We shall now contemplate the central panel.

The central panel of the Red Window

Keynote script: ***Ich schaue*** = ***I behold*** *(or, I am beholding)*

In this scene dynamics are presented which exist in the soul of the person who has attained to higher consciousness or 'initiation'. Included in the features here are some of the so-called 'chakras'. The term 'chakras' refers to energy vortices, or especially prominent centres in the aura; these are the soul's organs of perception. These vortices develop as a chasteness and wisdom, and a capacity for spiritual consciousness, develops in the soul.

The chakras

The person in this panel has developed some of his or her so-called 'chakras' or soul-eyes, through which higher consciousness can manifest. The chakras are rotating, wheel-like energy

---

[8] ΙΟΥΛΙΑΝΟΥ ΑΥΤΟΚΡΑΤΟΠΟΣ: ΕΙΣ ΤΟΝ ΒΑΣΙΛΕΑ ΗΛΙΟΝ ΠΡΟΣ ΣΑΛΟΥΣΤΙΟΝ.

[9] The Book of the Dead, trans. T. G. Allen, Spell 15B4 p 35, Univ. Chicago 1974.

[10] *Re-Atum Khepri Harakh-te* implies, "Sun god - Father god - morning Sun-god - Son of the sun (Horus) in east and west."

Central panel of the Red Window : *I am beholding*

centres in the aura, or soul. In Buddhism the Third Eye of Buddha represents one of these chakras. In the centre of this person's forehead there are two curved energy-waves. This represents the so-called Third Eye, a chakra which has two rays of energy.* This centre is developed by a program of spiritual study, including learning to discriminate between truth and illusion in many different ways, and by various kinds of meditating: an activity which Rudolf Steiner taught in a way suitable for modern times. Eventually the developed forehead chakra confers the blessed ability to commune with the higher-self consciously. This is nothing less than beginning the process of attaining to eternal consciousness. This same process therefore also means that the now clairvoyant meditant gradually communes with the divine-spiritual beings who have created our world.

At the throat area, there is a spiralling pattern, with 16 lines or rays of energy to it. This cognitional centre, or soul-eye, bestows further perception beyond that of the forehead centre. It grants perception into the thoughts of the Gods, or the 'Cosmic Thoughts', which in various systems of spiritual knowledge are known as 'spiritual laws' which sustain and develop Creation.* The exercises given by Rudolf Steiner to develop these higher faculties of cognition were designed for modern people, and are different to older systems of spiritual teachings.[11] The type of meditating he advises has the vital effect of stimulating, first of all, the forehead chakra into activity, before the other chakras are influenced into activity. This is essential if the experiences of the higher realities are to be assimilated rightly; in other words, it ensures that one is capable of maintaining one's ego-sense whilst in higher experiences. It is not surprising that when this heart centre is developed, it brings perception of the **emotions and feelings** of people, and other beings such as nature spirits. Hence the words in the middle section of the red window; "I am beholding".

In the area of the heart, and thus the heart chakra,* we see a dragon and a divine being battling each other. From a brief comment of Rudolf Steiner, it is the understood that the divine being here represents the widely revered archangel Michael. This archangel is referred to in many religious texts from Judaism and Christianity, especially in texts that deal with the theme of initiation, **which means the process of becoming a seer who can experience the spirit realms**. Rudolf Steiner explained, from his own extensive experiences of this archangel, that it is the great task and intention of this archangel to assist humanity to have an holistic or spiritual consciousness, starting with thinking spiritually rather than materialistically.

This means that a person has to realize that the spiritual side of life is very real, and to acquire understanding of spiritual truths is something which is important and possible for many people, even though to actually see non-material realities, one does have to be clairvoyant. The kind of spiritual thoughts that Rudolf Steiner provides in his life's work is a manifestation of the higher consciousness which modern people can start to achieve.

Sun and Moon

Now in the forehead area, associated with the two-rayed chakra, are some more intriguing features. It is clear from Steiner's original sketch that on the forehead, on the right side (the viewer's left) is the moon, with linear rays streaming out from it.[12] These straight or linear rays appear to represent the way that the moon's energies are perceived raying out from it, when experienced beyond the physical level. On the left side (the viewer's right) is the sun; this is hard to see in the carved glass, but both sun and moon are quite clear in our reproduction here, based on Steiner's original sketch.[13] The sun has curved or circular waves flowing forth from it; this represents the way that the sun's energies are perceived surging out from it, when experienced beyond the physical level. Notice that there is a spiritual being associated with the moon, who is looking backwards, whilst the spirit-being associated with the sun is looking forwards. The moon is known in anthroposophy as 'the gateway to birth', meaning that the soul on its way to re-birth descends from the zodiac stars to the outer planets and then to the moon, or the 'moon-sphere' as it called.

---

[11] My book, *The Way to the Sacred,* offers an in-depth guide to the process of spiritual development as taught by Rudolf Steiner.

[12] Schmelzer's view that the rays are drawing inwards prevents the moon from exerting any influence.

[13] Schmelzer & Glöckler, not seeing this, call the moon an object of "concentric arcs/rays".

Each returning soul has a karma, and their life shall be affected by what the 'laws of karma' require. The idea of 'karma' in anthroposophy is not quite the same as in Buddhism; the human being is seen as evolving in life after life, guided by a higher, eternal ego, which is active faintly within the everyday ego.[14] This is the outcome of its past life; for this reason the spirit being to do with the moon is looking backwards. Their influence is raying out onto the person, blessing the person's efforts to integrate what their karma, from their past life, requires of them. The influence raying out to the person from the spirit being of the sun, by contrast, is blessing (that is assisting and affirming) what the soul now is, and what that soul is striving to achieve in the future. For this reason the solar spirit-being looks forwards. Both spirit-beings are thereby helping the process of developing spiritual consciousness, that is, the third eye.

To achieve this initiatory step of awakening the forehead chakra, the person has to wisely unite the past with the present. Only in this way can he or she move towards their future potential. That is, whatever one's limits are in this life as the outcome of past karma, this has to be wisely correlated to what one wants to achieve. One's burdens, restrictions, obligations, abilities or lack of abilities, all have to be recognized and worked with. Within these limits, one strives to find or create opportunities for earnest spiritual development.

Saturn

The planet Saturn is shown above the head of the initiate. There are probably several reasons for this planet appearing here. The primary reason is to indicate the link between the human being and the solar system; to correlate the human being, and in particular a person on the path to self-initiation, to the spiritual influences coming from our solar system. This is quite clear from a section of a sketch in the Steiner Archives, from the time when Rudolf Steiner was developing his ideas for this window, see illustration 12, page 45. In this sketch, there are four depictions of the moon and the sun and Saturn in a straight line, forming a unity, and being influenced by a spirit being. But in the final sketch, and thus in the window, these three are grouped together in a kind of arc, and likewise they point to the link of our soul to the solar system. We have mentioned the link to moon and sun, in regard to the past and the future, but the sun also represents the ego or conscious sense of self, whilst the moon represents the temperament, the habitual ways of being.

In this context, Saturn represents the subconscious, wherein our deeper intentions or will exist, veiled from our ego; that is, from our normal sense of self. At this deep level, our will is an expression of the intentions of guiding beings from spiritual realms, reflecting the dictates of our karma. The person seeking deeper spiritual development needs to become perceptive to the subtle guidance from Saturn in respect of what karma requires. The influences of Saturn in the soul are manifested in our karma. These energies attempt to give us an intuitive sense about what our karma requires of us; they derive from the sublime beings known as the Thrones. But from Saturn, the spiritual person can also receive insights about what a higher Will, beyond one's personal karma, is seeking. Saturn is also positioned near to the place where the two 'spiritual ears' nearly join (see below), above the crown of the head. This could indicate that to become aware of the promptings and admonitions of the deeper guiding will from Saturn requires an enhanced inner listening capacity.

It is also the case that the chakra in the aura, above the crown of the head, referred to as the 'thousand petalled chakra' in Indian literature, is a Saturn-influenced organ of perception. But it is developed only at a very high stage of initiation, and Rudolf Steiner revealed little about it.[15] Saturn here can also be seen as pointing to this future chakra.

Spiritual hearing

On either side of the face there is a long shape, which almost looks like long curls of hair, which goes over the ears and descends down quite a distance. But each of these two forms also go upwards, and they nearly meet above the head of the initiate. They meet close to where the planet Saturn is shown. In contemplating these two things, I gained the impression that they are

[14] The concept of everyday ego and eternal ego or self is explained in the *Rudolf Steiner Handbook*.

[15] In a supplementary volume to the Complete Works, no.40, 1972, he indicates its existence.

‘ears’, that is, soul ears (or astral ears), meaning organs for spiritual hearing in the aura. This kind of ‘ear’ is to be found in ancient Celtic art, on their statues of gods or spirit beings; they usually extend up to the crown of head, but can also extend downwards, see illustration 5B. The term ‘astral’ means the soul, and ‘astral realm’ means the realm where the soul exists; so our soul or aura is an astral reality.

These ‘ears’ are especially relevant, as the initiate not only sees spiritual realities, but also hears them. And Rudolf Steiner has included two features about spiritual hearing that are very striking. Notice how on both sides of the face, near to the physical ears (not shown) there are two strange creatures. On the viewer’s right (on the initiate’s left), there is actually a bull, whereas on the other side of the face there is a lion. We know from the memoirs of Assia Turgenieff, that Rudolf Steiner told her that these two upright creatures are dressed in priestly vestments (clothing); and he stated, “They are whispering secrets of the cosmos into the hearing of the initiate”. What does this mean?

In anthroposophical teachings, as in earlier esoteric wisdom, such as the Mithraic Mysteries, a bull represents the sensual lower desires active in the soul (or ‘astral body’), whereas the lion represents these lower desires that have become ingrained and have taken hold of the life-forces (or ‘etheric body’). They are then quite aggressive and habitual, yet still can be somewhat veiled; that is, until the person is annoyed or aroused. This attitude derives from esoteric knowledge which was widespread in earlier times, about the inner link between these two animal species and the negative qualities in the soul, and also in our etheric body or life-forces. Apart from Mithraism, there are references to this in ancient Egyptian wisdom and in the Bible. For example, in a Psalm with esoteric qualities, King David laments that “Many bulls surround me, strong bulls of Bashan encircle me, roaring lions tearing their prey, open their jaws wide against me.” (Psalm 22:12)

But here the initiate, in seeking a purified, chaste spirituality, has overcome both of these negative influences. Therefore they are now fully metamorphosed, having been spiritualized, and as a consequence, they can now inspire intuitive understanding of the deeper secrets of the world. Knowledge of this secret of the esoteric spiritual life was known to a Medieval painter, Master Theodoric, who painted scenes in the extraordinary castle Karlstejn, located near Prague. Among the portraits of saints in this castle, are the four Evangelists – that is, those saints who wrote the gospels. Each of these has had a symbol allocated to him since very early in Christian art. The bull is the symbol of St. Luke, and the lion of St. Mark; but instead of just depicting these animals somewhere near the Evangelist, in this mystical castle these two animals are portrayed as if they have been tamed and have become totally obedient to the saint. This seems to me to be exactly the same dynamic as in the red window. One can see how the bull and the lion are close up against the ear of the their saint, as if whispering deep secrets of esoteric Christianity to them, see illustration 5A.

Now, at this point, you can read more about the deeper meaning of the features of the Red window, or just go to the south Green Window.

THE RED WINDOW: PART TWO

*** The forehead chakra**

This ‘lotus flower’ or chakra is developed through the kind of meditating Rudolf Steiner recommended, when in conjunction with this, a study program is also carried out. For this centre to develop, it is especially necessary that the seeker learns to discriminate between illusion and reality. Our soul or aura (or ‘astral-body’) is itself created from the spiritual energies of the sun and from the classical planets of astrology, as we prepare to incarnate. A developed forehead chakra is a Jupiter-influenced centre, and confers the ability to behold the soul world (or astral realm) and also to see the ether energies (the Ch’i or prana energy).

5A Above: St Luke (left) and St. Mark by Master Theodoric in Castle Karlstejn. He has depicted the bull and the lion as tamed and whispering into the ears of their evangelist.

5B Below: engravings of ancient Celtic deities from Germany, with astral 'ears'.
Left: from the old La-Tene Celtic period (ca. 450 BC); the ears reach upwards.
Middle: Mid-La-Tene Celtic (ca. 200 BC); extensive, emphasized astral ears on a deity, reaching both downwards and upwards.
Right: from the mid-La-Tene period; the ears of a deity reach upwards.

*** The throat chakra**
This is a powerful chakra, or organ for clairvoyant consciousness, and is influenced by Mars. This centre has 16 'petals' or rays of energy. Its development is assisted by deeper meditation and by specific soul exercises. In particular, it is developed by contemplation of what are called *The Beatitudes.* These are a series of especially deep sayings of Jesus Christ, reported in Gospel of St. Matthew, chapter 3, verses 3-11. It is also assisted by practising the six Parallel Exercises given by Rudolf Steiner (called 'Nebenübungen' in German), especially the **fifth one**, which focuses on open-mindedness. It also requires the virtue of not having a capacity to harm others by voice (or deeds, of course).[16] As is stated in the classic Theosophical booklet, *Light on the Path*: "Before the voice can speak in the presence of the Masters, it must have lost the capacity to wound."

*** The heart chakra**
The heart chakra is a sun-influenced organ, and has 12 petals or rays of energy. Once developed, it bestows perception of the emotive forces in other beings (visible and invisible), as well as perception of the nature spirits within plants and stones. It is also the 'soul-eye' or lotus flower that brings the ability to perceive etheric energies in minerals and plants; that is, it allows the person to inwardly sense the living elemental moods and dynamics of Mother Earth.

During meditation it can happen that one feels as if from every point of the body's periphery, energies are streaming in towards some central middle point. This middle point is the heart, (as Rudolf Steiner explained from an esoteric lesson on the meditation in 1910). There is a further development of this experience wherein one feels as if these energies are now streaming out, into the environment. The heart chakra brings to the meditant the kind of clairvoyance that bestows sensitive empathy with other beings, as distinct from perceiving their thought-forms. When we sense some subtle elemental quality, perhaps when walking near a flowering bush at sunrise, we sense it in the heart area rather than the head.

*** The Middle Beast: the anti-will forces**
The capacity that we humans have, as distinct from the animals, of thinking and for speaking our thoughts is described by Rudolf Steiner as a reflection of the Divine, as a sign of the divine origin of the human being; in particular, of the Logos, who spoke creation into being. This divinity is called the Logos, referring to the divine being mentioned in the beginning of St. John's gospel. So, the monster in this panel, who actually has no mouth or organs for speech, is not part of the divine power that has given human beings the capacity for speech. So this beast represents the 'Ahrimanic Double'. That is, the lower soul qualities that are associated with cold, hard, anti-social impulses, rather than with indulgent, self-centred 'luciferic' temptations. Such a negative quality in the soul could separate off a human being, in the future, from all that which we could achieve spiritually by allowing the Logos to gradually come to manifestation in us.

This middle beast is also a force that blocks the highest of the three levels of spiritual consciousness. Rudolf Steiner calls this level, "Intuition", but the word here has a different meaning to the usual meaning of this word in English, which is, a semi-psychic awareness of something. The process of attaining this third level of initiation consciousness is due to great spiritual beings, called the Thrones, who manifest their intentions through this Saturn influence.

Note: Fear and Hate are interconnected states of soul; wher e there is fear of something, there is also some hatred of it, and vice versa. So the middle beast of anti-will or Hate, is also about fear of the Spirit; and the stunted creature on the right, expressing Fear, is also about hate of the Spirit.

From here, imagining that we are in the Goetheanum, we turn to our right, and go over to the south Green Window. (We shall consider the sequence of the pathway from window to window, at the end of our explorations.)

[16] A guide to these exercises is given in my, *The Way to the Sacred.*

The south Green Window

And the light of spirits, it became the light of human beings

And human love comes into being

The love in the cosmos is efficacious

And human love takes hold of him

THE SOUTH GREEN WINDOW

Colour Overview
What is the significance of the colour green for the soul? How does it subtly convey the message of the two green windows? Rudolf Steiner stated in regard to this colour,

> If one lives into the green of Nature, if one sinks into a sea of green, then one attains an inner strengthening of that which one actually is, in this earthly life. Our earthly incarnation is strengthened or affirmed, our normal every-day ego is enhanced.[17]

The meaning of these words becomes clearer when we consider blue, and especially purple, because these two are inwardly associated with the non-physical, the spiritual aspect of life. In essence Rudolf Steiner is saying here that green, which is the background colour to the plant realm across the Earth, represents our earthly personality. That is, the mixture of soul qualities, both good and bad, that we manifest in our life here, in the physical plane. So the two green windows will depict the nature of the primary challenges facing a person who seeks to develop their higher-self.

Thematic Overview: this was described in a script written by Rudolf Steiner on the sketch:
Und das Licht der Geister / Es ward das Licht der Menschen
And the light of spirits, it became the light of human beings

We shall explore the meaning of this over-script below.

A brief overview of the scenes
In the **left** panel: a venerable man in a devout activity, and above twelve faces surround a person.

In the **central** panel: three divine beings rising up to the spiritual sun, viewed by a human being who is consumed with passion.

In the **right** panel: a column within a large column, and above, the single person has awakened.

Exploring the south Green Window

Left Panel

Keynote script: ***Und Menschenliebe entsteht*** = ***And human love comes into being***

To understand the very relevant message of the central panel, we need to see just what the left panel and the right panel are saying. What we see here is a venerable man, whose clothing and body gesture indicate that he is involved in a religious or spiritual activity, perhaps in a temple of some sort.[18] Above this person, we see the face of a person, who is surrounded by twelve replicas of himself. There are also rays of energy streaming upwards to this face, from the person below.

There are two important features in this panel, which we have not yet mentioned; the twelve small faces are clear, and quite prominent, and the large face in the midst of these has its eyes closed. To understand this scene, we need to note the differences here to what we see in the right panel. In the right panel, these two features are reversed. The twelve small faces have faded almost away, and the eyes are open in the larger face. In addition, in the right panel, the energies raying upwards are now reversed, they are now streaming downwards. To find out what these panels are really saying, we need firstly to explore the central panel, and then we can return to the two side panels.

---

[17] Lecture 1st Jan. 1915 in GA 291, ps. 102-3.
[18] For those who are aware of a minor reference to the ancient Persian sage Zarathustra in regard to this panel, this is commented on in Part Two.

The central panel of the south Green Window

Keynote script: ***Die Liebe der Welt wirkt* = *The world's love is efficacious***

or ***The love within the cosmos is efficacious***

(The word 'efficacious' means 'to be actively exerting an influence'. A rough translation is, 'works'; thus, *The world's love is working.*)

So the script here is saying that the divine love-force subtly permeating the world or the cosmos, from the Creator, is now actively affecting this person. The three spiritual beings ascending upwards, are manifesting this divine love-reality. They are Angelic beings, who exist in this divine, chaste purity. But now we need to consider the being referred to as "Lucifer" by Rudolf Steiner, the being who leads his 'luciferic' hosts of helpers. To achieve a sense of ego is essential for human beings, and indeed this is the underlying purpose of higher divine beings allowing such 'fallen' deities as Lucifer to exert an influence in the evolution of the human life-wave. This on-going inherent process actually began long ages ago, and is referred to in the Bible as the 'Fall of Man'. * For Licifer is that spirit being who in the Lemurian Age, began the process of inspiring a sense of personal ego in human beings. This ego-sense is primarily achieved through romantic-sensual activity and also through having one's own thinking – which however Lucifer wishes to have human beings manifest as naïve, ungrounded thinking and self-centred opinions. As Rudolf Steiner emphasizes, a person seeking spiritual development needs to conquer the power that these ego-centric states exert over the soul, so that a higher ego-sense can be born.

In the first of the four 'mystery' dramas which Rudolf Steiner wrote, *The Portal of Initiation*, a character representing Lucifer tells a meditant, *"Spirits desired in you to follow only their own will; {but} I gave you your own will."*[19] These words indicate the role of this untruthful, but not really evil being, who opposes and slanders higher divine spiritual beings. Over the ages, Lucifer has gradually instilled a personal ego-sense, and continually supports this in humanity. (The fully evil being is Satan or 'Ahriman'.) All of this is part of a plan from much higher, divine Powers, to help human beings, once they have a clear ego-sense, to become ethical individuals.

Because of a misunderstanding, this central panel has been described as depicting Luciferic spirits. This view sees the three spirit beings in the central panel, whom I regard as actually divine Angels, rising up into the heights, as Luciferic beings.[20] I see the other view as the result of students of anthroposophy being influenced by some words in a document dating from 1917, which regards these beings as "luciferic spirits". But this document is **not** from Rudolf Steiner; it was written by an artist, F. Siedlecki, whose task was to supervise the work to be done on the windows, at the building site. He had to create a diagram of the layout of the windows in the hall, and indicate which artist would be working on each one. Siedlecki later carved his own version of the windows, but his version ignores or alters several features in Steiner's sketches, (see below, purple window north).[21]

Certainly the south Green Window presents a message about the influence of Lucifer, however we shall soon see that it not depicting 'luciferic' spirits, but rather, holy angelic beings. So, what is the window depicting, what is its message ? Two commentators concluded that the human being here, although he is being consumed by fiery desires, "is being torn away from the Earth" by three 'luciferic' fallen spirits; these beings "want to tempt him away into radiant-illusionary realms".[22] But neither the south nor the north Green Window is about the evolutionary past of humanity. They are about how a spiritual seeker of today can move towards spirituality, towards a better future. So this window is giving us a message about how the **result of** Lucifer's influence **can be overcome**; and also **that noble beings are there to help the seeker**. Thus, it is not so much about how personal, self-centred sensuality and illusory yearnings arose, but how the

---

[19] From the Portal of Initiation, Scene 4.

[20] Earlier booklets have such comments as, "In the south window Lucifer appears (through the three Angels), who wants to release the human being from the earthly gravity..."(M.Glöckler), or "we see...the danger of being lured away by the light" (A.Schmelzer).

[21] He was Franciszek Siedlecki, writing on 3rd March 1917; in "*Die Goetheanum Glasfenster*", Rudolf Steiner Nachlassverwaltung, Dornach, 1996, p. 103.

[22] Schmelzer and Glöckler, respectively.

spiritual seeker **can move towards overcoming this emotional condition**, as part of the quest for self-initiation. This is precisely indicated in the 'gesture' of the venerable man, when contemplated in conjunction with the script for the left panel, "*and human love comes into being*".

This person is gaining a new perspective about their normal every-day self, in particular about emotions, feelings and yearnings; not so much their thoughts and will (these are the theme of the north Green Window.) For the person on the path to self-initiation it is crucial to become aware that their normal emotions, feelings, and wishes are imprisoned, or tainted, by ego-centric, illusory yearnings. Therefore this person is depicted as being amidst a burning fire. The entire gesture of this panel is saying that the meditant is now **at the point of seeing through** the illusions in their emotions and desires, derived from Lucifer. Hence what was previously considered to be quite acceptable, indeed very desirable, and a source of pleasure, now is seen to be too sensual, too illusory, too self-indulgent, and dependent upon transient sense-world stimuli and sensations.

Indeed this person is now experiencing that the most potent pleasures - and this does not mean **joys** - are actually like a burning fire to the soul. Until the heart is purified, the scorching flames of such pleasures are not perceived, because one's body or the world, always offers opportunities for gratification. And it is precisely awareness of this dynamic that the person here is experiencing. He or she is feeling that they are on fire, and the fire is deriving its force from the lowly part of the body.* And it is just this lesson that the gesture of the noble Angels are pointing out to this person, by their objective presentation of the joy and tranquillity that holiness and chasteness brings. The spiritual seeker here is clearly experiencing the contrast between his or her own fallen human condition and that of the Angels, who embody the Spirit-self, and who assist the seeker to develop this quality.

Moreover, the flames around this person have a resemblance to a burning bush; and this may be intended to remind the spiritual seeker of the extraordinarily important event in the life of Moses as told in the Bible, in the Book of Exodus. In this event, Moses perceives what looks like a burning bush, although since it is a spiritual (clairvoyant) phenomenon, the bush is not actually burning. There comes the awe-inspiring moment when from this bush, the deity who is to give Moses his mission, announces Its name in a complex Hebrew phrase, which is normally translated as *"I am that I am"*. Rudolf Steiner teaches that this phrase is indicating that the human being has potentially an eternal, higher ego, and that this is also part of God's own being and means "I am *the* I am". We can note here that this translation is of necessity slightly simplified, as the Hebrew verb used here refers to both the past and the future, all in the one word; this implies that the higher, true ego or "I" is beyond the flow of time. (We explore this further when contemplating the north Purple Window, p. 67) The carving in this window is a powerful statement as to how strongly the person experiences, on their spiritual path, a demand made on them for purity, if he or she is to move towards an ego-sense which is to incorporate the high reality of the eternal 'I am'. * (Such a person could be called an 'acolyte': the classical term for someone who is a student on the spiritual path. Since meditation is so important in this process, such a person can also be called a 'meditant'.)

So we see before us a person having a very important spiritual lesson. His or her attempts at becoming spiritualized are having an effect; spirituality is really emerging, and therefore bringing this potent life-lesson. This level of spiritual development is understood in anthroposophy as the beginning of the "Spirit-self". This means that the soul or aura (or 'astral-body'), with its capacity for thinking, feeling and will, is becoming more refined; and it also means that their actual higher ego, their Spirit, is being formed, as well. But at first this brings some painful life-lessons. Our spirit has its own aura, called the 'Devachanic' aura in anthroposophy. To learn more about the soul aura and the spirit aura, see my *Rudolf Steiner Handbook*, or if you are familiar with anthroposophical ideas, see the relevant sections of Steiner's book, *Theosophy*.

To understand more about this experience, we firstly need to know that the spiritual seeker is not left alone on the path, for Angelic beings, who are an expression of what in Christianity is referred to as 'the Holy Spirit', endeavour to grant some awareness of the blessed joy that exists in the higher worlds, and which the human being who develops purity, can share in. So, here the person is beholding three blessed, divine beings, presumably Angels, all of whom are directing the attention of the seeker to the spiritual sun. In contrast to Luciferic beings (or fallen Angels) these beings are not looking at the person, not trying to influence him in a way that would make him un-free. Instead they are serenely, joyously, modestly embodying the divine, here represented by the spiritual sun. And the acolyte is realizing that this is the state of consciousness to which he or she should be striving.

The acolyte realizes that with these divine angelic beings, there is a cosmic or spiritual source of warmth and light which envelops them in tranquil joy, and carries them ever onwards and upwards to the Spirit – and this source is the spiritual sun. Luciferic spirits have a different appearance * and would be focussing on the person, drawing her or his attention to an illusory Paradise state of being. Moreover, it is not only that the spiritual sun is the focus of these divine beings, and which is depicted in many of the windows. For the aura of the uppermost Angel is shown as inherently belonging to the spiritual sun, because it actually has rays that are reaching up to the sacred spiritual sun. This feature is unique to this window. (We can note here that the number of rays from the spiritual sun varies from window to window; I have concluded that the number of rays from the sun in any window has to do with the artistic balance of the scene, and is not connected to esoteric symbolism.)

There is then another, very important dynamic shown here, indicated by the script of this panel: *The world's love is efficacious.* For the great message of this window is that the meditant is being made aware of the fact **this same warmth and light that exists in the Angels, exist in his or her own soul – but as a burning fire** ![23] That is, in these divine beings, those very same forces are present which are in the human lower-self, but in the imperfect human being they burn and deceive; however in their un-fallen, original condition, they are a source of joy and purity.

This is the meaning of the script of this panel, namely the spiritual seeker is becoming aware that the power of Love in creation is a glorious, primary element of the divine beings who created and seek to nurture humanity, but this same power, due to the age-old influence of Lucifer, is a destructive burning fire in his or her own soul. This 'fallen' situation is necessary, and part of the plan behind the creation of humanity. Long ago, human beings were primitive, coarse entities, with a primitive and illusory sense of self. But human beings have to evolve upwards from a lowly ego-sense to eventually attain a higher-self. So here the acolyte is having the priceless lesson from Angels, that his or her lower-self is a degraded expression of the same light and warmth that blesses divine beings. How does the person in this panel, attain to this insight? The left panel has already indicated this; it is by making the effort towards a way of life which assists the purification of the emotions, and arising above a self-centred, indulgent way of thinking and desiring. The right panel then indicates what the blessed results are for those who make this effort.

The right panel of the south Green Window

Keynote script*:* ***Und Menschenliebe ergreift ihn = And human love takes hold of him / her***

What do we see here ? The person shown in the left panel has disappeared; in their place is an ornate pillar ! But also, above the pillar, as we noted earlier, the larger face now has its eyes opened, and the surrounding twelve smaller faces have faded. The message is very inspiring in regard to our connection to, and experience of, the zodiac. The twelve smaller faces represent the zodiac energies which help form the matrix of our spiritual nature. Rudolf Steiner refers to the zodiac as forming our sense of "I" or ego. This teaching is especially relevant to our higher-self, for as Rudolf Steiner taught, "we human beings can know the zodiac through having {deep experience of} our ego".[24] He comments further that, "the ego has twelve aspects to it"[25]; and through our various incarnations in different zodiac signs, the human being does indeed gradually form a twelve-fold quality to his or her individuality.

---

[23] As Rudolf Steiner explained, in GA 266c, (p 230) for example.

[24] GA 170, p.128,132.

[25] GA 119, p.228.

In this connection, when speaking of ancient spiritual practises, he told an audience that when an acolyte was to be led out into the cosmos in an initiation ritual, twelve priests gathered around the person to support their ego, or sense of self, as he or she entered into the cosmos. But in the modern path to self-initiation, the meditating person should have developed enough ego strength, when they are in meditation to be able,

> to experience the zodiac energies as flowing through the ether, and as something that is not raying out into the vast universe but instead, is raying down towards their own self, striving to form into a centre {in one's soul}.[25]

What these words are teaching is directly depicted in this window. With the zodiac influences forming a background to our consciousness, it is as if we have an 'un-awakened' greater dimension to our self, or one could say, the potential to develop this higher ego. So here in the **left** panel, it is depicted as if this greater self is literally un-awakened, that is, asleep. But in the person who attains to initiation, the purity of the soul **can encompass and integrate this higher-self**; so in the **right** panel, its eyes are opened, and the surrounding nurturing matrix of zodiac influences are fading away.

We can note here that there are nine rays going upwards to the un-awakened higher-self as the acolyte develops spirituality, and also in the right panel, nine rays are going down from the now awakened higher-self. But this number has no esoteric significance; for Rudolf Steiner actually sketched six rays for the left panel, and a collection of rays for the right panel which merge with each other, and hence cannot be separately counted. The artist had obviously found that nine forms a satisfactory artistic balance here.

Consequently, the rays of energy which were raying upwards, as the human being worked towards developing this higher-self now stream downwards. That is, influences from the person as they began to consciously strive towards spirituality, helped to form their higher-self. Now, in the right panel, the awakened higher-self can bless and transform the human being; hence it now rays influences, associated with the zodiac, downwards towards the person. The meditant finds that their capacity for intuitive insights grows. And the result of this transformation is shown in a remarkable way. The person has become a pillar ! But in fact, very significantly, this pillar is set within a larger pillar, which is less visible, being of a paler colour. This beautiful image is telling us that once you start to develop the higher-self, then you become part of a wider spiritual reality, greater than just your own self; you become part of a spiritual community.[26] And since these two pillars are of the same kind as were in the first Goetheanum, then the pillars are part of a building which is a kind of temple.

This symbolic temple is many things. Firstly, in the world, it is the community of souls who are devoted to spirituality – in whatever way that may be, such as personally in meditation and spiritual study, and vocationally in uplifting, holistic work in the world of many kinds, in Steiner-related circles this will include Steiner education, and its holistic healing modalities, or farming bio-dynamically; but there are many other activities too. But there is also a second, deeper, aspect to being part of this 'temple'. In spiritual worlds there exists, for souls who really seek to develop spiritually, a kind of future home.*

The base of the column also has a specific form; it is the same as one of the seven huge pillars in the great hall; the so-called Mercury pillar. It is my conclusion that the word 'Mercury' here does not refer to the planet Mercury, but to one of seven evolutionary phases presented in anthroposophy, known as the Mercury Age. This Mercury column is very significant here, because it is saying that the successful spiritual seeker can attain that special achievement which life in our times is offering; namely what Rudolf Steiner calls 'Michaelic thinking'. What does this term mean? The Mercury Age began about 8,000 years ago, it includes our current age, and goes on for a considerable time into the future. The highest attainment in this Age, from the viewpoint of modern humanity occurs when human beings develop, supported by but transcending their own logical capacities, an intuitive, insightful consciousness (or thinking).[27] It is this kind of spiritual

---

[25] GA 77b, p.63-65.
[26] The suggestion (G. Hartmann) that this is showing a second etheric spinal column is unconvincing to me.
[27] As explained by Rudolf Steiner in GA 89, p.73.

thinking, or holistic consciousness which is meant by 'Michaelic thinking'; a consciousness ennobled with help from the archangel Michael. The last words from a meditative verse by Rudolf Steiner express the result of this state; "Blissfulness draws into me, the blissfulness in which *the soul finds the spirit.*"* He means here a quiet inner joy which arises through such actively achieved insightful consciousness, not through an ungrounded, ecstatic experience.

Part Two of our commentary on this window follows, or you can move on to the North Green Window.

SOUTH GREEN WINDOW: PART TWO

*** The 'Fall of Man'**
The epoch in which Lucifer accessed the human soul and brought about the 'Fall of Man', was the Lemurian epoch. This event is referred to in the Bible, in Genesis, chapter 3. Rudolf Steiner explains that it was in mid-Lemuria when humanity underwent a 'fall' or descent out of a purely ethereal realm, and the associated consciousness, into matter, that is physical existence. This event began the long journey of the soul, requiring many lifetimes, to evolve up to the Spiritual-self condition. As I mentioned in the *Rudolf Steiner Handbook*, this was some 18 million years ago; this entire drama is explained in detail by Rudolf Steiner in his book *An Outline of Esoteric Science.*

*** Deriving its force from the lowly part of the body**
The positioning of the burning flames, indicates that the lower sensual passions are a major part of the challenge the acolyte is now facing, since being chaste is a primary quality in the spiritualized human being.

*** How far the un-spiritualized human being is from this great reality of the eternal ego**
The statement by God to Moses in the burning bush is in effect saying, as Rudolf Steiner taught, "I am **the** I am". In other words, the higher ego of the human being is God, or derives from God. The term 'God' here means an interweaving of two of the seven Powers or 'Elohim', namely Yahweh and the cosmic Christ. This statement to Moses is very significant for the spiritual seeker, as is the associated teachings about the true, higher ego, or Spiritual-self from ancient Egyptian esoteric wisdom, which calls the Spiritual-self, 'Isis'.[28] The words of Isis, formulated in ancient Egyptian times, but preserved in Hellenistic Greek by the priest Plutarch, is "I am all: that which has been, that which is, and that will come into being; no mortal man has ever lifted my veil."[29] That the earthly ego-sense has to transform up to a higher, eternal ego-sense, or "I", is indicated in a brief document, called "Credo", written by Rudolf Steiner at the age of 27, "Destroying all self-centredness, this is the foundation of the higher life. For whoever lets this selfhood die, shall find an eternal existence. That which is mortal in us in our separate-self." [30] By "separate-self" here is meant the illusory, ego-centric sense of the "I" or the ego.

*** Luciferic spirits have a different appearance to Angels**
Quite apart from the clearly modest, selfless gesture of these three Angels, Rudolf Steiner depicted Luciferic entities as having no lower part to them, in his pastel drawing, "*The Mensch im Geiste*" (*The Human Being in the Spirit*). Their 'body' starts in the chest region and they have broad, outstretched wings. Also, as he wrote in one of his personal notebooks, their wings commence in the throat area, and not from the back.[31]

*** The soul finds the spirit**
These words are from a profound meditative verse on the spiritual dynamics of the Mercury Age, in which we now are living. It is a prayerful verse to the Logos, or sublime spiritual being, who brings into manifestation the will of the First Cause or actual Creator,

---

[28] The Egyptians also used this same word to refer to various divine beings who provide the matrix of the Spiritual-self; but as Steiner taught, "Isis", after the Egyptian epoch, means the Spiritual-self, not a goddess.

[29] Plutarch, ΠΕΡΙ ΙΣΙΔΟΣ ΚΑΙ ΟΣΙΡΙΔΟΣ, cap. 9, p.14: ἐγώ εἰμι πᾶν τὸ γεγονὸς καὶ ὂν καὶ ἐσόμενον καὶ τὸν ἐμὸν πέπλον οὐδεις πω θηντὸς ἀπεχάλυψεν.

[30] From *Credo* published in the Complete Works, vol. 40. p. 274.

[31] Beitrag no. 19 to the Complete Works, p. 4.

Great, encompassing Spirit,
In thy being's cognizing *(Erkenntnis)*
is cognizance of the cosmos, (*Welterkenntnis*)
which is to become mine.
Thou art.
I will to unite my soul to thee.
May thy cognizing Guide illumine my pathway.
I travel the path of life, feeling thy guide.
Thy guide is the life-Sun:
it lives in my yearning;
I will absorb its being into mine.
Thou art.
May my strength absorb the power of the
Guide into itself.
Blissfulness draws into me –
the blissfulness in which
the soul finds the spirit.
Thou art.

*** A kind of future home**
The indication of a great temple to which the successful spiritual seeker may belong, also has other, more esoteric meanings. Novalis, the pen-name of the poet Friedrich von Hardenberg (1772-1801), in his exquisite poems, "Hymn to the Night" refers to a kind of spiritual temple in spirit realms, where those who serve Christ may find themselves after life on Earth has ended. Rudolf Steiner, in his Mystery Plays, refers to sacred temples of the initiates existing in spirit realms.

And the deepest of all such references is to be found in the Book of Revelation, where Christ Jesus himself states; "*Him who overcomes I will make a pillar in the temple of my God.*" (Rev. 3.12) The right panel of the south green window is directly alluding to this lofty and inspiring statement, also. We can note here that the words "*him who overcomes*" (*῾Ο νικῶν ποιήσω,*) is actually using the verb which was used in ancient Grecian culture, when referring to someone being initiated. (The second part of Revelation 3:12, goes on to refer to even higher esoteric secrets, discretely indicating that the long pathway of many lives can, for those who truly achieve high goals of spirituality, draw to a close, "*Never again will he leave it".*)

*** Zarathustra and this window**
Those readers with knowledge of anthroposophy may have heard that this venerable figure is Zarathustra; this is a distraction from the deeper meaning of this window. For more about this see the Appendix.

Reviewing the over-script:
As we saw earlier, the over-script of this window is:
Und das Licht der Geister / Es ward das Licht der Menschen
And the light of spirits, It became the light of human beings

In other words, the influence of Luciferic spirits brought an awareness into primitive human beings, and this lit up a dim ego-sense in them. The message of the window is, that the normal ego-sense for human beings is partly enveloped in an illusory, self-centred sensual tendency – and this is now incompatible with the spiritual goals one is aiming for.

The spiritual seeker's task is to retain, of course, the sense of "I", but to lift this sense of "I" up, so that it is enveloped by the higher ego, helped by the Angels, and through cleansing the emotions of the intense sensuality and self-centeredness which Lucifer brings.

Now we walk over to the north Green Window.

The north Green Window

And the Spirit of Heaviness gathered the opposition and there developed resistance in the human will

The will is being born *The world actively effects my will* *The will is born*

THE NORTH GREEN WINDOW

Thematic Overview:
There is an over-script to this window written on the sketch by Rudolf Steiner,

> ***Und der Geist der Schwere sammelte den Widerspruch, und der ward in der Menschen Wille Widerstand.***
> ***And the Spirit of Heaviness gathered the opposition and there developed resistance in the human will.***

Brief overview of the scenes
In the **left** panel: a human being standing between light and darkness, arms outstretched, and underneath him or her, three unpleasant beings are moving up towards this person.

In the **central** panel: an extremely striking scene, a human being up high, gazing at a truly remarkable winged entity, which curves around in a serpent-like manner.

In the **right** panel: the human being is now free of the power of the three entities, who are sinking down deep into the Earth.

Exploring the north Green Window

Left Panel:

Keynote script: ***Es gebiert sich der Wille = the will is being born***

This window is about the thinking and the will qualities of the spiritual seeker in terms of the influence of the body on the soul; whereas the opposite window, in the southern wall, is about the emotions or feelings. There is a 'weighing down' of one's consciousness which occurs from the interaction of the body and soul. This is of course triggered off by the process of being born, for as Rudolf Steiner explains, in the pre-conception phase, we have a cosmic, imaginative consciousness, not a logical mind which uses mental images derived from the sense world. This side panel is bluntly depicting the inner un-freedom, and the lack of spirituality of the soul because thinking and the will are often naturally earth-bound and self-centred. Contrary to what one would think, there is no sun depicted in this window.[32] For the artist who carved these windows, Assia Turgenieff, reported that Rudolf Steiner explained to her that **there are two moons here**,

> These forms are two aspects of the moon; the one glitters, the other flames. The first strengthens the memory, the other exerts an influence on the instincts.[33]

What does this extraordinary feature mean? How can there be two moons? The answer is, because there are two aspects of the moon: the malignant and the wholesome aspects. To those who go on the modern path to spirituality, which in the deeper sense of Rudolf Steiner could be called 'self-initiation', this esoteric truth is not difficult to understand. Firstly, the moon governs our life-forces (or 'etheric body'); this is responsible for the healing and maintenance of the cells of the body. It is also the force behind our perceptions. All sense impressions are sustained within its network of subtle energies, and all clairvoyant impressions are conveyed to our awareness by this life-force body. It is also the force behind the capacity for reproduction. The moon also is placed in a zodiac sign (not constellation) when we are born, and the psychological qualities of that sign thereby become embedded in this life-force body; and this dynamic gives us our 'temperament', that is our predisposition.

It is in our temperament, or semi-conscious psychological drives, that lowly instinctive desires and self-centred urges and attitudes hide; these are a formidable part of the ' lower-self '. When it

---

[32] Contrary to what all four earlier booklets about the window say, including the 'official' books from the Goetheanum by G. Hartmann and A. Schmelzer, the human being here is not positioned between the sun and the moon.
[33] Assia Turgenieff, *Die Goetheanum Glass-Motive* Dornach, 1935, p.17.

comes to the demanding path of spiritual development there are obstacles that the seeker has to overcome. But firstly one has to be conscious of them these obstacles; they tend to hide themselves. For example, one becomes aware of how meditation hardly ever happens, despite our clear intentions to do so; or how often lowly impulses surge around the soul, just when the attention should be focussed on a sacred topic. Another problem is how instinctive is the urge towards a subtle egotism, a self-centred way of approaching other people, or in one's own spiritual quest.

The source of these obstacles lie partly in the etheric body (or life-forces), that is, in our habitual, semi-conscious ways of being. And it is precisely all of this which malignant lunar energies try to strengthen by becoming active in one's etheric body. So the moon has both wholesome and malignant energies associated with it. Rudolf Steiner has therefore placed two moons in this scene. In it, we see 'ahrimanic' lunar sprites endeavouring to exert an influence in the semi-conscious predispositions. These are the two aspects of the moon, and we see how the stars or planets are lined up on the border between darkness and light; this indicates how the soul is awkwardly balanced between these two.

The central panel of the north Green Window

Keynote script: ***Die Welt erwirkt den Willen* – *The world actively effects my will***

In other words, 'the Earth has an effect upon my will', or, 'life in the physical world is efficacious for my will'.

My conclusion here is not consistent with what the four earlier publications state. These writers all conclude that this panel is depicting the evil being known as Ahriman. However to me, it is depicting a profound truth about the 'ahrimanic double', but also that high, divine beings are required to work with, and to regulate, how this lower aspect of human nature affects each person's karma. This is similar to the companion Green Window where indirectly, the effects of Lucifer are depicted, but along with the efforts of divine beings to help the meditating person to overcome that. A particular influence of the ahrimanic energies in the lower-self is the focus here: namely deadened, materialistic thinking and self-centred, anti-social intentions. To conquer these qualities, the spiritual seeker has to:

1: acknowledge the existence of these tendencies.
2: understand how these forces in the soul are linked to the solar system.

Through this the spiritual seeker comes to understand a rudimentary meaning of the ancient expression: "as above, so below", as we shall soon see. Now, we have already seen that the side panels make it clear that this window is about becoming free; free of the semi-conscious predisposition towards materialism and a hardened, selfish will. To appreciate the tremendous spiritual depth of this scene, some knowledge of earlier esoteric wisdom (called 'Mystery streams' in anthroposophy) is helpful. In Part Two of this section, more shall be said about this figure. In this earlier part, we are trying to find out just what kind of being, and what kind of negative qualities the seeker is experiencing here.

Firstly, we need to note that the human being is **not** on a mountain ! All earlier commentators on this scene state that the person here is on a mountain, amidst trees; but this is an error, as we can know from Rudolf Steiner's own words. He explained in a lecture about this scene, "I don't know why on these rocks, one has drawn trees; for I have drawn **leaves**, real leaves."[34] The difficulty in understanding what the scene is about, has led to his words being ignored by all other writers in the windows.[35] So here we are **not** seeing a person high up on a mountain side amongst trees; rather we are simply seeing leaves. But, leaves lying on soil, which itself is piled up high. What then does this unusual feature really mean?

[34] From GA No. K 12; Die Goetheanum Glas-Fenster, 1996, Dornach, p. 49.
[35] Schmelzer has tried to partly acknowledge Steiner's words, saying "on a mountain amongst shrubs and leaves".

Being enlightened
To answer this question, we need to know that we human beings, in the physical world exist within what in anthroposophy is called 'the physical-etheric body'. So in anthroposophy, what is normally called the 'body', is more precisely thought of as a physical organism which is permeated by an etheric organism, or life-forces which maintains its existence; hence the term, 'the physical-etheric body'. So, if a person is symbolically placed up high, but just on leaves and soil (not on a hill), then this scene is a metaphor or poetic way of saying, that this person **has reached the pinnacle of spiritual thinking, but** as a person **still in a physical-etheric body**. In other words, the person in this window panel is experiencing intuitive insights; that is, spiritual, holistic understanding, or wisdom. To achieve even higher insights, the person would have to really transcend their body powerfully, through higher consciousness states, in effect, clairvoyant states obtained virtually outside the body. Having an intuitive insight is not usually a clairvoyant experience, although here in this panel it is.

This person, at the heights of intuitive, earthly consciousness whilst in their body, is being 'enlightened'; he or she is enveloped in lightning-like flashes. The reason for this is, that all thoughts have an astral radiance in them, for thoughts come from the soul, or from higher realms into one's soul. They are not the by-product of the brain. As Rudolf Steiner taught,

> Astral light and thoughts are the same reality, seen from different sides ! In so far as we live in thoughts, we live in {astral} light. When one observes thoughts with clairvoyant capacity, then one sees the thought-element as light.[36]

Flashes of Insight
But to have such a powerful esoteric enlightenment as this person is having, his or her soul will have been blessed with help from the archangel Michael. This archangel is one of a small number of archangels who are referred to esoteric literature; seven of these archangels are associated with one of the seven classical planets. Rudolf Steiner explains that Michael, known in ancient times as the 'sun archangel', is crucially important in the modern path of self-initiation, for it is this archangel who strives to assist people to think spiritually. Also, he is the sun archangel, and therefore close to the great sun god, or cosmic Christ spirit;

> The forces of Michael are connected with the Sun, the energies {of this archangel} remould the brain subtly {of those who seek to understand anthroposophical thoughts}, and this can allow lightning-like illumination-thoughts to occur; these reveal the deeper aspects behind the natural laws.[37]

But in this state of enlightenment, who is the serpent-like spirit-being the initiate is seeing, and what are the dynamics which belong to this being? If you have some awareness of ancient esoteric wisdom, perhaps from your own studies, or faintly felt from a previous life, then this figure may be strangely familiar and also startling to you. All the previous booklets on this theme are not helpful here, as they have concluded that this being is Ahriman. One author commented about the seven planets here, enveloped in the body of this winged serpent, that these were not planets, but "represent time and space – experienced by people as little wheels".[38]

But in fact the seven round globes in this panel are indeed the seven planets: the Moon, Venus, Mercury, Sun, Jupiter, Mars, and Saturn. We know this to be the case, because their names are written by Rudolf Steiner on the sketch used by the artist[39]. This fact, that the body of this winged serpent encompasses the seven planets, **is of enormous significance for those who seek spirituality**. But before we discover what these planets mean here, we need to unveil the nature of this winged serpent.

The winged serpent
To discover the secret of this image, we need to draw on initiation wisdom, from both anthroposophy and the Hellenistic world. Firstly, this being is not Ahriman, for two reasons, at

---

[36] GA 291, p.115-6.
[37] Lecture, 12th May 1913.
[38] M. Glöckler, Die Glasfenster-Motive des Goetheanum.
[39] The sketch was published by Rudolf Steiner Archives in *Die Goetheanum-fenster*, p. 19, 1996.

least. Firstly, Ahriman's face has been carved by Rudolf Steiner in wood, and it is completely different. Secondly, in speaking with Assia Turgenieff, he said these decisive and remarkable words to her,

> This being is indeed a great, lordly spirit-being; his image must have dignity and a **sublime-lofty quality**.[40] (*Emphasis mine, AA)*

So, these high words refer to a divine being, not to 'Satan', known as 'Ahriman', in anthroposophy. So what kind of being is this, and what is the message of this scene? Let's be quite clear that we see a winged serpent, whose influence encompasses the solar system, and whose sphere of influence extends down to the Earth. What Rudolf Steiner has achieved here is a masterly image, which combines two deeply esoteric images from antiquity, but which have been metamorphosed, so that they become meaningful to people in today's world, who are interested in spiritual development.

In the initiation wisdom of the Hellenistic Age, in Gnostic sacred art, a serpent entity is often depicted, who has seven rays on his head, and who also has a lion's face. This being is called Chnoubis or Chnoumis, and appears to be originally an ancient Egyptian god called Kenmut, see illustration 8. But, a profoundly significant feature here is, that a number of these images have the inscription, **"I, even I, am the Good Spirit"**, (in Greek the *"Agathadaemon"* which means 'noble and good spirit'). So here is a presentation of the malignant (serpent) and also the holy, involving a serpent with seven rays from his head. The seven rays on its head, instead of the seven globes along his body, is an earlier way to indicate the planets. We shall see that the serpent-like being in the green window in this scene is a new version of this Chnoubis entity, but intermingled with **another entity**. Before we consider the second spirit entity interwoven in this serpent-like figure, let's explore this Chnoubis entity a little more, through the striking pendant in illustration 8.

The larger pendant has writing around its edge, which indicates that it was important either for esoteric contemplation, or was thought of as imbued with magical powers. The deity is lion-headed and has the seven rays which represent the classical planets, and there is an inscription around his head which reads "Chnoubis". It also has the moon and a star, and possibly the sun. Around the outer circle are the names "IAO", Abraxas, Michael and "Sabaoth". * The name IAO was used to indicate a human being whose spiritual development has taken him or her into a close relation with the Divine; and 'Sabaoth' refers to 'hosts' of divine spiritual beings.

That the pendant has the moon and a star, and possibly the sun, indicate that Chnoubis was understood as a being involved with our soul forces, which are linked to the planets in the solar system. Regarding the term IAO, Rudolf Steiner taught that "in IAO, the Seraphim, the Cherubim and partly the Thrones are active,"[41] and that "these letters are the unpronounceable name of the secret god...the god from whom the "I am" comes .[42] So the figure of Chnoubis is very deeply significant. It is a meditation on the earthly ego-sense and how it is potentially a divine "I". It is also a meditation on the human soul as having within it, planetary forces, whether noble or debased – just as astrological wisdom confirms.

That Rudolf Steiner had a very high view of the best of the ancient Gnostics wisdom is clear from his various comments. But his positive comments do not refer to the Gnostics who were opposed to esoteric Christianity or denied some of its core elements; for example, those Gnostics who decided that Jesus was not actually incarnate, but existed simply as a ghostly entity. Rudolf Steiner's high praise of the insightful ancient Gnosis is clear from such comments as,

---

[40] Assia Turgenieff, Die Goetheanum Fenster-Motive, Dornach, 1935, p.17.
[41] GA 265, p. 460.
[42] GA 265, p. 215.

8 CHNOUBIS

Left above: A Roman gold & heliotrope magical pendant, from ca. 300AD.

The deity is lion-headed and has the seven rays which represent the planets. It also has the moon and a star, and possibly the sun. These indicate that Chnoubis represents our soul forces spread out over the solar system.
The inscription has the name Chnoubis around his head. Around the outer circle are the names Iao, Abraxas, Michael and Sabaoth.

Left below: a Hellenistic amulet showing a lion-faced entity with seven rays. The sigils carved on either side indicate it was used for magical purposes, such as healing.

> the students of {*what was the equivalent of*} anthroposophy in the early Christian centuries, were the Gnostics.[43] One can regard as 'Gnostics' all the writers of the first centuries of Christianity, who sought the deeper, spiritual meaning of Christian teachings.[44]

Amongst these people he included Clement of Alexandria and his student Origenes.[45] Consequently, it follows naturally that Rudolf Steiner could design esoteric artwork that was inherently linked to some elements of the ancient Gnostic wisdom; although the old Gnostic artwork would be somewhat metamorphosed. Now to consider the second spirit being or esoteric image from antiquity which is integrated into the winged serpent in the green window.

In the Hellenistic Age, in the profoundly esoteric religion of Mithra, there were depictions of a stern, rather ominous deity, who had four wings, (as the serpent in the Green Window) and who was encircled six or seven times by a serpent, see illustration 9. (The name and meaning of this deity is unknown, but it is referred to as either 'Saturn', 'Zervan', or 'Aion'.) Also, concerning this deity, there is the same significant feature as with Chnoubis. Although this being has a fierce lion face, other Mithraic carving depict a metamorphosed version of this grim deity. Such carvings show a person or a deity, who has a serpent coiled about him, but a small lion face in his middle parts, and this being is noble-looking, and empowered, see illustration 10.

Rudolf Steiner commented on Mithraism, with the startling statement that it was clear to those initiated in the Hellenistic Mysteries, "in Jesus of Nazareth, Mithra was present" He also stated that the person who was initiated into the Mithraic religion, {in the event of them being baptised by John the Baptist}, at the moment of baptism knew that, "Mithra can become born in human nature !"[46] These striking comments are indicating that the religion of Mithra revered the same divine being as the Christian religion: Jesus Christ. But these statements indicate that the initiated priests of Mithraism perceived the Christ as a being who still existed in spiritual realms, who was not yet incarnated. Supportive of Rudolf Steiner is the fact that the surviving texts and artworks of this Mithraic religion are, in part, very similar to that of Christianity.

So, Rudolf Steiner regarded the Mithraic wisdom as deeply valid, as a kind of pre-Christian manifestation of the vessel of Christ, and therefore inherently linked to the esoteric Christian wisdom of anthroposophy. This means that his esoteric artwork could indeed have an inner similarity to that in the Mithraic-Gnostic wisdom. We shall see more evidence of Rudolf Steiner's artwork echoing directly ancient esoteric artwork, when we explore the north Purple Window. There he affirmed the accuracy of ancient Egyptian wisdom by incorporating esoteric artistic imagery which directly echoes the artwork from about 2,000 BC. In addition, Rudolf Steiner designed an item of jewellery directly incorporating ancient Egyptian esoteric art.

As these Mithraic drawings show, carvings of this being in his negative mode, depict a lion-headed entity holding a sceptre or staff, indicating that he has authority, see illustration 9. The gesture of this body gives the impression that he is guarding or blocking the path. (In the large image in illustration 10, this entity also has symbols of various planets close to him.) Also, the serpent goes around him six times, which appears to represent six planets, and then it comes up over the back of his head, making a seventh stage.

On his chest are various planetary symbols; these include thunder-bolts, which are associated with Jupiter, and a rooster, which is a symbol of the sun. He also has the staff of Mercury (or Caduceus); and there are iron implements, which is a metal associated with Mars,[47] and there is a pine-cone which is a symbol of Venus. His left hand may hold a symbol of the moon; it is not clear what this is. He holds in his right hand a large key which twelve little holes in it, representing the zodiac. (The other smaller drawing is included to show variations on this theme; in this version he is standing on the Earth.) So this is an unpleasant winged serpent with planetary features.

---

[43] GA 56, p.20.
[44] GA 8, p.153.
[45] GA 52, p.408.
[46] GA 131, p. 27-28.
[47] Usually associated with the mythological being called Vulcan, who is associated with Mars in the myths.

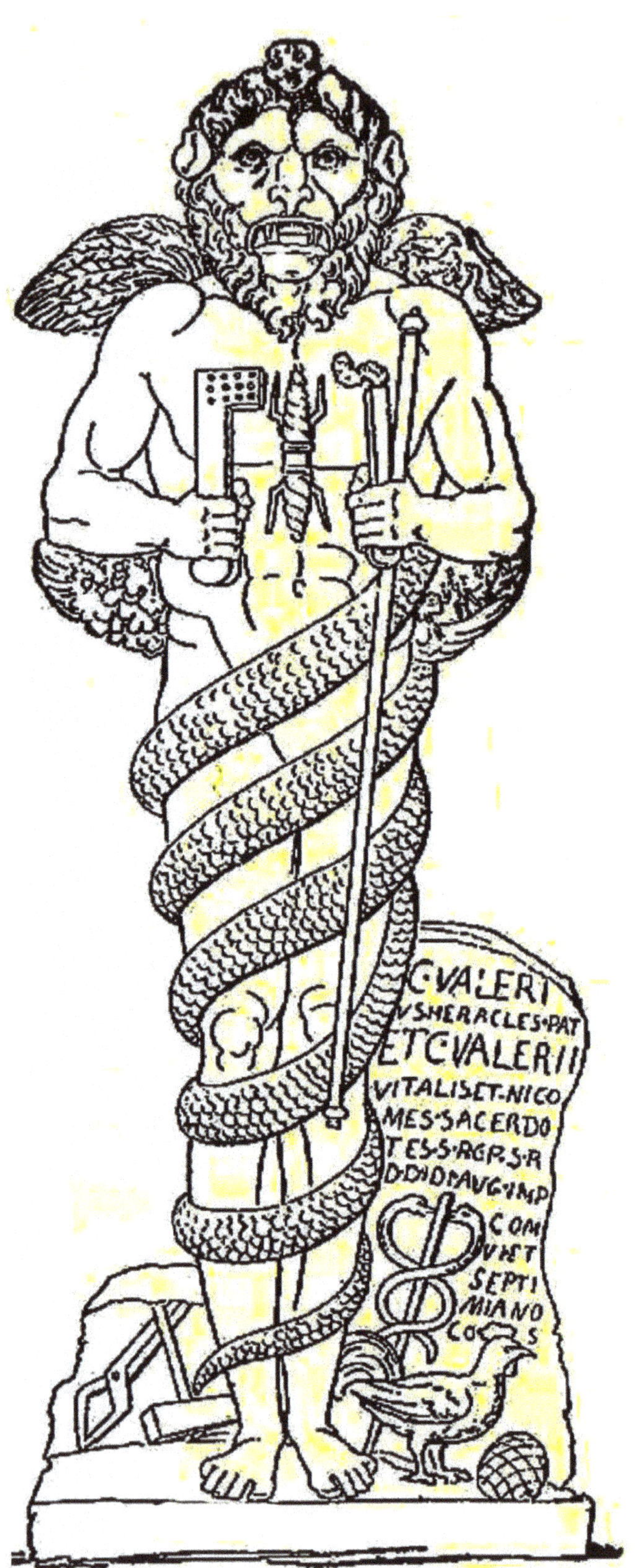

9 The stern guardian: Two drawings of ancient Mithraic statues, showing the stern role of this Guardian in permitting and also monitoring the shadow-side of the planetary forces in the soul. (The inscription notes that the statue was set up by Gaius Valerius Heracles, a Mithraic high priest.)

The carving of the noble-looking Mithraic deity however, shows that this being is quite closely connected to the lion-faced deity. But unlike the negative being, there are only a few planetary indicators in this carving. The thunder-bolt, a symbol of Jupiter, is there, and significantly he holds this in his right hand; a sign of having empowerment over Jupiter forces (which bestow wisdom on the soul). And the moon is there, in sickle form, directly behind his head. This seems to indicate a victory over the negative lunar energies – just as suggested in the right panel of the green window. Also, the head of this deity is especially emphasized, for he has firstly, a lot of wavy hair, but he also has rays of energy streaming out from the head – very similar to the person in the central panel of the window, in their moment of 'enlightenment'.[48]

In the light of anthroposophy, a Gnostic attitude that this serpent-like being is only a malignant creator, is seen as the result of an incomplete view of creation. There is a higher, noble aspect to the creation of the physical, mineral world. The Mithraic attitude, which has resulted in carvings of two beings, a stern repelling being and a noble one entwined with a serpent, and usually with four wings, is much more accurate. For although matter is a lowly reality, compared to the higher realms, and a realm in which malignant influences can gain access to the human soul, there is a divine plan behind the creation of matter. The creation of inert matter and the placing of human beings in the physical world with a lower-self, is due to the activity of much higher, divine beings who intend that human beings shall work their way up out of a lowly state, and eventually attain spirituality.

The twofold esoteric artwork from the Mithra cult and the Chnoubis serpent, have been integrated in a metamorphosed way into the Green Window's winged serpent. This figure speaks of a high deity that has both an ominous and a noble role. What is this role? This four-winged serpent, enveloping the seven planets, is an entity representing the subtle and complex role that various divine and malignant beings have in the task of bringing about the malignant side of creation, which is connected with human beings and their lower-self. This mystery is reflected in the character of Mephistopheles, in the great play written by Johann Wolfgang von Goethe, called *Faust.* Mephistopheles says,

> I am a part of that Power which constantly wills evil, but constantly creates the good.
> Ich bin ein Teil von jener Kraft die stets das Böse will und stets das Gute schafft." (lines 1336/7)

Mephistopheles is not the same as the winged serpent in the glass window, but a lesser malignant being, whose words indicate the complexity of the role of 'fallen spirits' in the evolution of humanity. With the gnostic Mithraic artworks, there is a grim being who guards the divine realms from human beings who are as yet unworthy; and yet this entity also metamorphoses into a divine being, or declares that it is itself a divine being. We can conclude that this metamorphosis occurs to the same degree that the human being becomes spiritualized. So the winged serpent in the green window, appearing to the acolyte in her or his moment of enlightenment, is in effect a combination of these two entities, of Chnoumis (Chnoubis) and the unnamed dualistic Mithraic entity. This entity is saying: behold how your lower-self is interlinked with the seven planets; I must be a guardian, blocking your entrance into higher realms, but yet I want to reveal just what in you needs to be refined. Hence this serpent has qualities similar to what Rudolf Steiner calls 'the Greater Guardian' in his book, *Knowledge of Higher worlds, how is it attained*?

So it appears that the ominous lion-faced deity has a similar function to the serpent of the green window, portraying the human being's lower-self in planetary symbolic terms. The associated Mithraic carving of a noble entity and the inscriptions on Gnostic gemstones, portray what Rudolf Steiner was hinting at, when he said that the serpent being has a "sublime-lofty quality". The implication here is, as the spiritual seeker ennobles their soul, then this being transforms into a reflection of one's now developed spirituality.

---

[48] This figure also has three animal forms across its middle part; on his right (our left) is a goat's head, in the centre is a lion, and on his left is a ram's head. These details are not relevant to our theme.

10 Mithraic deity: a cosmic reflection of the ennobled soul qualities of the acolyte.

So the winged serpent with four wings in the green window, enveloping the seven planets, is in effect a combination of the un-named serpent-entwined deity of Mithraism, whose sanctuary was placed at the end of a chamber with seven portals, and also the Gnostic-Egyptian deity, Chnoumis, the serpent with seven planetary rays. The significance of these two deities is unclear to scholars, no doubt because they derive from such secret initiatory knowledge of antiquity. *

To understand the over-all message of this green window, we need to note that in the two side panels, the malignant sprites each have a face similar to that of the serpentine being in this central panel. As we have just noted, malignant influences are associated with this "*great Lordly being, who has dignity and a sublime-lofty quality*". The acolyte, in this moment of enlightenment regarding his or her own thinking (and will), has perceived two potent facts. One is, as we noted earlier, that the lower-self is not just threefold (negative thinking, feelings and will) but is sevenfold, because our soul or astral body is formed by the seven planets; as esoteric wisdom of astrology reveals.

The other fact is that there exist a great, majestic being who is required to allow malignant, Ahrimanic entities to maintain the lower-self of the person, and thereby to potentially undermine the spirituality of the human being, especially in regard to thinking and will. But this being also ensures that this challenging situation **does not continue**, **once the human being makes progress on the self-initiation path.** It acts as a kind of guardian or overseer. So these sprites in the left panel want to reinforce the materialism in the thinking and lethargy in the acolyte's will, with the result that the effort to really have a spiritual way of thinking about the world, and undertaking spiritual development exercises is just too hard, takes too much effort.

In this dynamic, the stern, majestic spirit-being has to ensure that a human being does not attain to spiritual seership, and does not become free to cross over the 'threshold' between the physical world and the spiritual realms, and experience these realms in full consciousness, **until** that person has overcome materialistic, body-burdened ways of thinking and self-centred intentions and habits. This experience presents important knowledge of the **sevenfold lower-self** to the acolyte.* Until the spiritual seeker has really earned that great privilege of being consecrated to sacred spiritual goals by transforming their sevenfold soul, the pathway across the threshold into the higher realms remains barred to him or her.

So until the spiritual seeker is spiritualized and purified, this lofty spirit being appears to be a malignant power; but once there is sufficient spirituality, this being becomes a helper who opens the doorway. By then, the lowly sevenfold reality (the shadow in one's own soul) has become noble and good. Knowledge of just what mixture of noble and of lowly energies are in one's soul, is revealed by interpreting the horoscope, using a deeper, esoteric astrology. But such astrological work does have to be done with wisdom and spiritual knowledge, as Rudolf Steiner emphasized. The author's book, *Horoscope Interpretation – a Rudolf Steiner Approach*, the only such book written from anthroposophical knowledge, provides a basis for this serious work.

So in this panel the seeker is having a moment of deep insight or illumination; she or he has realized something very significant. This person has seen how their soul has a cosmic aspect to it, for it is deeply linked to the planets in our solar system. But he or she has also perceived that this fact has to do with the lower-self or the so-called 'Double', in a significant way. The meditant has realized that there is a negative, unpleasant shadow-side to their own soul, which owes its origin to energies raying-in from the 'dark side' of the seven classical planets of astrology. They have experienced the 'sevenfold lower-self'. Rudolf Steiner only spoke about this theme once, but it is depicted here in this green window.

The seven planets and the winged serpent, or the shadow side of the soul, astrologically

Horoscope interpretation in the light of anthroposophical wisdom is so valuable that we shall consider here are a few examples of the sevenfold lower-self or Double, as revealed in the horoscope, when it is interpreted with insight.

Moon in Opposition to the Ascendant
'Unresponsive life-forces weaken the sense of self'

With this aspect, the temperament is blocked from resonating with the Ascendant which is a kind of secondary ego-sense (or 'ego-reflection' point), and hence this person seeks emotional support from others, becoming too interwoven with friends. This person seeks excessively for an inner link to others. The mother's influence is very important. This person may seek a mothering partner if their mother was a failure...

Venus in opposition to Mars
'The driving force enflames feelings and desire'
This aspect produces intense emotions and strong desires. It also produces the choleric personality, and hence relationships are often stormy, alternating between like and dislike. This person is often emotionally immature...

Venus inconjunct to Mars
'The driving force intensifies self-centred feelings'
This aspect, similar to the Opposition, causes excessively self-focused desires and feelings, and constantly going between liking and dislike, as well as a strong sensuality...

Mercury in opposition to Mars
'The intellect is unclear and aggressive'
This aspect is a primary factor in creating the choleric person. That is, someone who is combative, argumentative, always ready to defend their situation and wishes, and who often has strong ambitions. This person says the wrong thing at the wrong time, and can have rash thinking. Their ideas often illogical if they have to debate anything when angry. They can be fault-seeking, but they do like mental challenges. This aspect often occurs in charts where the south node is in Sagittarius...

Mercury to Neptune
'The intellect is enmeshed in fantasy'
With all aspects involving Mercury and Neptune, the intelligence is affected by spiritual influences crossing over 'the threshold', that is, raying in from spiritual realms and influencing the logical thinking. So with a conjunction, thinking is very imaginative; the person can be subject to delusions. The fantasy life is strong, and there is an artistic sensitivity. In a more negative chart: a state of psychic confusion exists regarding the soul-life of other people; their mental images come inside one's own mind. There can be tendency towards lying...

Jupiter opposition to Saturn
'Unwise thinking and blocked intuition undermine confidence'
With this aspect Jupiter's clear thinking and Saturn's intuitive sense of one's life-path mutually block each other. So there is inner conflict and contradiction, and a lack of confidence. These lead to actions which don't yield worthwhile results and take the person into a path that is not helpful to their purpose in life...

Also, the horoscope, anthroposophically interpreted, reveals much in regard to the position of the planets in the zodiac signs, for example:

Saturn placed in Pisces at birth
With this, the gentle, sensitive, and often psychic, Piscean person is dampened right down. Piscean people respond to the subconscious admonitions from Saturn, about sensing and then being true to, their destiny (or karma), in a way that makes them fearful of life. For the Piscean translates these solemn and earnest promptings into a need to be very cautious, to refrain from asserting oneself. This is because the Piscean's sense of ego is usually not strong, so she or he easily surrenders their own wishes and becomes obedient to authority. They can be fearful and moody, and with their emotional life under pressure to be self-restricting, inclined to make a poor choice of partner. (From the *Horoscope Handbook - a Rudolf Steiner Approach*)

There are also much worse personality traits revealed by the horoscope, which need not be detailed here. The four wings indicate that the seven soul qualities, including the negative ones, from the dark aspect of the planets, also exist in the life-forces or 'etheric body'. There are four kinds of life-forces that form our etheric body, not just one.

The right panel of the north Green Window

Keynote script: ***Es ist der Wille geboren = The will is {now} born***

This panel shows the underlying relation of the human being to the ahrimanic sprites from deep inside the Earth, once he or she has succeeded further in their spiritual striving. These sprites now have to give up trying to induce a spiritual lethargy and self-centred tendencies in the will; and a subtle materialism in the thinking. There is no pathway for them up into the human being. So the person is now shown as walking towards the positive, wholesome lunar influences. Behind her or him, the negative lunar influences are weakening, but wholesome lunar energies are growing stronger.

In the current Goetheanum, the carving of these negative energies is somewhat stronger, and placed nearer to the head of the person than in the original sketch made by Rudolf Steiner. The original sketch shows a smaller, darker moon, in its waning phase; from which several, not very prominent, energies are raying out towards the acolyte. How it was appeared in the first Goetheanum is unknown, as apparently there are no photos of this window from the first building. The way the five stars (actually, planets) form a bridge across to the positive lunar energies indicate that the soul of the person is now inclining towards the good; it is no longer balanced precariously between the malignant and the good. A way to overcoming these more hidden, subtle negative qualities is indicated in a long, core meditation text from Rudolf Steiner called *The Foundation Stone Meditation.* We cannot go into the details of this extensive text, but there is a section in the third part of the text where these words occur;

> **Human Soul** !
> You live in the resting head,
> Which, from the foundations of Eternity
> Discloses for you the Cosmic Thoughts:
> **Practise Spirit Beholding**
> In serenity of thought,
> Where the eternal aims of the Gods
> Bestow on your own I
> The light of Cosmic Being
> That the will may be free.

These words are revealing that through diligent meditation, and heart-centred study of spiritual truths, the meditant gradually achieves a high goal of spiritual development, namely freedom in the will. Freedom here means unhindered ability to be ethical, to have spirituality; as explained by Rudolf Steiner in his book, *The Philosophy of Freedom.* But since the will is mainly subconscious, it is interwoven with the semi-conscious urges in our temperament; these words imply that by absorbing spiritual wisdom and making this live in one's heart, the veiled negative qualities are driven out. (See my *The Foundation Stone Meditation – a New Commentary* for a careful translation and brief, meditative commentary on the verse.)

NORTH GREEN WINDOW: PART TWO

* **Mithraic deity (**Zervan, Aion, Ialdabaoth**)**
Some scholars consider this Mithraic deity to be closely linked to a Gnostic deity called Ialdabaoth. There are a number of other deities from antiquity which reflect this same wisdom; they are entwined by a serpent, and also have four wings, such as Saturnus-Aion has. It is significant that Ialdabaoth is described by Plato as a creator god, with good intentions, yet in later Greek texts, this being has acquired a malignant quality, becoming an entity who created the material world, which is viewed in Gnosticism as a negative, un-spiritual reality. Looking again at illustration 9, it is worthwhile to consider the question, just why was a serpent used in so many ancient esoteric groups? Rudolf Steiner explains this is a very earlier lecture in 1902, from which his book, *Christianity as Mystical Fact*, was written,

> The serpent symbolised the process of initiation. The snake was viewed everywhere {in esoteric religions or groups} as a valid symbol for the developing of the spiritual capacity {in human beings) which occurs by being 'drawn through matter' {the material, physical world). The snake {symbolizes the process of} making possible the destruction of the last manifestation of the matter {the matter-bound state of consciousness}.[49]

So, the snake is an unpleasant creature, and as such it represents the lowly ego, or earth-bound self. But when the intention arises in a person to transform themselves into their higher self, this occurs when we are here on the Earth, in a material, bodily state without which the human being cannot have a life. Without this life on Earth, spiritual development is not possible. The snake is a symbol of the lowly material condition, but this is also the condition out of which a person can arise and overcome their lower-self, if such a decision can occur in a person's earthly consciousness.

This same perspective underlies the magnificent and profoundly esoteric fairy tale by Johann W. von Goethe, *The Green Snake and the beautiful Lily.* One of the early great seers of ancient Greece was Helenos, son of Priamos and Hacabe. A tradition in ancient Greece recounts that already as a child Helenos received his clairvoyant capacities, and that this happened when he was within the temple of Apollo Thymbraios. A very esoteric symbolic statement has survived about this initiate. It is said that "he had slept there overnight, and when his parents came in the morning to collect him, they saw that the holy snakes had cleaned the points of entrances to his sensory organs with their tongues."[50] In the light of anthroposophy, these "points of entrances" must refer to the ether body, as all perception, both of the physical sensory organs and from the soul (its chakras), is mediated to a person by the life-forces which are interwoven with the sense organs and the chakras. The tradition appears to be saying that the overcoming of the lower-self, that is, of engaging with the lowly qualities and transforming them (a process symbolized by a snake) leads to higher consciousness. So the snake is a symbol of the lowly material condition, but it is also the means by which a person can overcome their lower-self.

*** The Guardian and Christ**

Considering Rudolf Steiner's words that the Christ is an aspect of Mithra, one can see that the carvings of a noble deity in the Mithraic temples, and the inscriptions on the Gnostic gems, are indicating truths compatible with Rudolf Steiner's teaching that the Greater Guardian being is an aspect of Christ.

*** The seven planets**

In only one of his thousands of lectures did Rudolf Steiner speak about this, and what he taught then is of profound value. From the brief notes of this lecture that have survived, we learn that those who seek to transform their soul, with its seven-fold planetary qualities, substantially improve the experiences that occur in the after-life journey. But in addition, a very deeply esoteric matter is glimpsed in the brief notes of this lecture; it concerns our impact on the planetary spheres, The audience in this lecture were given to understand that such personal development also has an impact on the planetary spheres themselves: their malignant nature is lessened. This is a profoundly significant theme, which expands our view of our relationship to the solar system in a dramatic way.

The Double is sevenfold, because we derive our aura or soul from the seven 'planets' of the solar system; and as astrological wisdom makes clear, each planet has an evil and a noble side to it. To achieve this, knowledge of our horoscope, in the light of anthroposophical wisdom, is essential as it reveals both conscious and subconscious imperfections present in the aura, from the planetary spheres.

---

[49] Archive manuscript, lecture, Berlin, 29th March 1902: "Die Schlange gilt überall als Symbol für die durch die Materie sich hindurchziehende Entwickelung des geistigen Lebens. Die Schlange vermittelt die Vernichtung der letzten materiellen Manifestation... ".

[50] Article, *Helenos*, in the Pauly Encyclopaedia of Antiquity.

Reviewing the over-script

As we saw earlier, the over-script is:
Und der Geist der Schwere sammelte den Widerspruch, und der ward in der Menschen Wille Widerstand.
And the Spirit of Heaviness gathered the opposition and there developed resistance in the human will.

We can see now that the message of this window is that Ahrimanic powers have brought about impediment to the spirit in human beings, but the spiritual seeker, recognizing these hidden forces, must become free of this, and gain permission from a Guardian to achieve access to divine realms.

From here we walk over to the south Blue Window.

The south Blue window

Willing

Making a decision *The external environment resolving* *He has willed*

THE SOUTH BLUE WINDOW

Colour Overview
What is the significance of the colour blue for the soul? Here are a few core comments from Rudolf Steiner in regard to this colour,

> Blue encourages the impulse to overcome the earthly ego qualities, and to develop piety, devoutness; in the colour blue, the cosmos gives us a divine compassionate blessing, it reaches out to us in blue.[51]
>
> As astral clairvoyance develops, a delicate heavenly blue shimmer begins to appear to the meditant. ....in blue rests the **yearning** of the spirit. [52]
>
> .....if one is immersed in blue, one feels the need to overcome egotism in oneself.[53]

Thematic Overview: Rudolf Steiner wrote one word for the theme of this window:
Wollen = **Willing**

The key features of the scenes
In the **left** panel: a man is walking along a track with a gun, looking for a bird to shoot. Above a spirit being is handing over a bird to another spirit being.

In the **central** panel: we see twelve various images of the zodiac.

In the **right** panel: the hunter actually shoots the bird.

Exploring the south Blue Window

Left Panel:

Keynote script: ***Sich entschliessend*** = ***Making a decision***

We see a hunter walking along, intending to shoot a bird, and above, in the upper right, the group-spirit of that bird species is handing over one of its birds to the guardian Angel of the hunter. The over-script of this window is "willing", and the script for the left panel is "*making a decision*". So this panel is pointing to the destructive nature of the un-spiritualized will inside the human soul – and the impact that such an urge has on the other living creatures. It also is poignantly speaking about the dynamic in which the animals (or their group-souls) find themselves. They have to allow themselves to be sacrificed to the disharmonious urges in human beings. *

Now, instead of leaving the right panel to the last, we shall consider it next.

The right panel of the south Blue Window

Keynote script: ***Er hat gewollt*** = ***He has willed***

Here we see that the hunter has killed the bird. Rudolf Steiner asked the artist to ensure that the bullet be made clearly visible in the carving. The group-soul of the bird has no option other than to hand over this member of its flock (which forms a small part of its being) to the human. The lesson here is quite blunt, about the kind of aggressive urges that exist in the soul. The lesson of both the left and right panels is to be found in a deep consideration of the central panel. The

[51] GA 275, lecture, Jan 1st 1915.
[52] GA 291a, p. 224 and p. 207.
[53] GA 191, Jan 1st 1915.

person seeking spiritual development needs to become aware of these deeper instinctive forces in the will, and feel the urge to counter them. This task is helped by a contemplation of the central panel.

The central panel of the south Blue Window

Keynote script: ***Die Aussenwelt im entschluss = The external environment making a decision/resolving*** (or, '*the external world*' *making a decision*)

This central panel consists of twelve images of the zodiac, but these are unusual images which, separately, and also all together, have a powerful message for the viewer; so let's explore them. Rudolf Steiner pointed out that the gestures of the arms and body in general, of the human forms in these images, are not connected to the eurythmy forms for the zodiac signs; they are, he said, "purely will-associated movements".[54]

PISCES
The most prominent image in the blue window is the one for Pisces; it is at the bottom left-hand corner. This prominent position means that this series of zodiac images starts with Pisces; this is because the northern hemisphere is currently in the Age of Pisces. This image shows the Earth down below and then the moon, next to which are the two fishes of the traditional Pisces symbol. Above is a human being with the stars of Pisces shown outside this figure, and also in the part of the body which the constellation of Pisces governs.

With the moon underneath the feet of the person, it is as if it is under the power of the two fish; these of course represent the qualities of Pisces. The image of the moon under one's feet is found in the New Testament, namely in the book of Revelation, where it represents the overcoming of the lower-self. The moon symbolizes an earlier evolutionary phase (called the old Moon aeon) during which a base, primitive astrality came into humanity. In the Gospel of St. John, the remarkable scene is given at his depiction of the Last Supper, of the washing of the disciple's feet by Jesus. This event is teaching a lesson about the humility and sense of service needed by those who are in authority, spiritually.

ARIES TAURUS GEMINI
We then move up to the image for Aries and to the next one, Taurus, and above that, Gemini. These three images are entirely different to that of Pisces; they are straightforward depictions. But each of these indicate a part of the human body, for the stars of that constellation are placed in the relevant part of the body, as well as outside it. This feature reminds the viewer that our body has been fashioned by the spiritual beings (Gods) from zodiac energies, over long ages. And each image includes a small depiction of what part of the body the sign is related to: a ram for Aries (which forms our head), a bull for Taurus (the neck and shoulders) and a second person for Gemini (our arms and hands).

CANCER
But when we look a little further up, at the image for Cancer, we see a very different scene. In addition to a person with the stars depicted outside and inside, there is also a prominent symbolic form. It is a wonderful metamorphosis of the traditional double-spiral symbol for Cancer. It also has some similarity to the thoracic cage, which is the area of the body that Cancer governs. This cage is the series of interlocking rib bones that protect the organs in the upper trunk of the body. Spiritual beings, operative from Cancer, have formed the thoracic cage. *

[54] A.Turgenieff memoirs, p. 18, 1935.

LEO VIRGO LIBRA
Now slowly moving down the right side of the scene, we again encounter three traditional images: Leo, with a lion and the stars outside and inside (it governs the heart); Virgo with its stars (it governs the stomach), with a feminine figure holding her traditional sheaf of grain. Thirdly, we see Libra with its stars, and an unusual graphic which is a freely interpreted depiction of some of the bones in the hip area which Libra governs, alluding to the body keeping itself balanced. The shape of this skeletal feature also has a slight resemblance to the traditional symbol for Libra. Moving further down the blue window, we come to Scorpio.

SCORPIO
From Scorpio on to Capricorn, the images in this window are about what happened in the evolution of humanity in remote Ages (for full details of this, see my book, ***The Lost Zodiac of Rudolf Steiner – Exploring the four sets of zodiac images designed by Rudolf Steiner***) Briefly put, in an ancient Scorpio phase of our evolution, primitive humanity, after having emerged from a primordial aquatic existence, and become air-breathing, split into the two sexes.[55] The image here shows, as with the other eleven images, a human being with the stars outside and inside. But here also an unpleasant astral creature is depicted, which seems to be moving towards the person in a somewhat threatening way. This is a depiction of the Double or lower-self, even though the creature is not actually a scorpion, the usual symbol of (lower) Scorpio energies.

SAGITTARIUS
In the image, we see a human being with the stars outside and inside. But behind this person also, is positioned an unpleasant etheric or astral entity, similar to a centaur. The centaur is, in Rudolf Steiner's teachings, a deeply malignant being; it is how the lower-self or Double appears, "it is an etheric being...it is equipped with all the savage instincts of the animals".[56] So in this image, another way of depicting the lower-self is presented; and it was in the earlier part of the Lemurian Age that the Sagittarian phase of our evolution took place. So this image, like the one for Capricorn, alludes to the Double, and in particular, the Age when this was taking further hold on the human being.

CAPRICORN
In the Capricorn image, we see a human being with the relevant stars outside and inside. It was in a remote Age, prior to Lemuria, known in anthroposophy as the Hyperborean Age, that the Capricorn phase of our evolution occurred. It was then for the first time, that matter began to incorporate itself into the tenuous physical-etheric body of human beings. Behind this person is positioned an unpleasant sprite, or similar being, from the elemental world: that is, an etheric or astral entity. When Capricorn is the sun-sign (or the rising sign, to a lesser extent) then that person has a strong ego-sense, and hence, if not a somewhat evolved soul, has self-centred, hardened ego qualities.

AQUARIUS
Finally, we come to the image for Aquarius, at the bottom right side of the window; in contrast to all other scenes here, this one is about the near future. It shows a human being with stars outside and inside, as seen with the other zodiac forces throughout this window. But in addition here we also see a baptism scene; someone is baptising another person who appears to be partially immersed in water. This immediately reminds us of the New Testament event where Jesus was baptised by John the Baptist, in the river Jordan. But looking at the image carefully, we now note that the second person, the one being baptised, is not actually immersed in the water, in the way that is done in a religious baptism rite; this person is in water only ankle deep. The ankles are the part of the body governed by the forces streaming in from Aquarius.

---

[55] This phase occurred during the second half of the Lemurian Age.
[56] Lecture, 6th Nov. 1917, in GA 178.

Now, Aquarius is an **air** sign, not a water sign, however water can symbolize the ethers, which also flow and surge and swirl, in a manner similar to water. So we can conclude that this scene does allude, in the first instance, to the task of John the Baptist, in baptizing Jesus; but it also points towards the great future mission for John. Rudolf Steiner taught that it will be his task, in the next zodiacal Age, which is called the Sixth Post-Atlantean Age, to 'baptise' people into the Christ-light by helping them to become sensitive to the ethers, to receiving the Christ-Word as it resounds in the ethers. This Age commences in AD 3573, and is also called the Aquarian Age. It will lead humanity further towards a true individual ego-hood of a 'Christed' nature.

This central panel is providing two powerful lessons about the will. Firstly, the divine, selfless will, or creative intentions, of the high spiritual beings whose influences raying in form the zodiac, are operative in humanity's evolution throughout the Ages. Their will is a selfless, self-sacrificing one, in which they pour out their energies and wisdom, in order to bring humanity into being. Secondly, it is pointing out how much is still unredeemed in the hidden part of the will, and also how the ahrimanic Double came into the human being. In my book, *The Lost Zodiac of Rudolf Steiner -Exploring the four sets of zodiac images designed by Rudolf Steiner,* there is substantial information about these symbols, how they tell us about the influence of the zodiac in the evolution of humanity, and also the twelve meditative verses Rudolf Steiner wrote about our personality, from the point of view of our sun-sign.

SOUTH BLUE WINDOW: PART TWO

*** The animals and humanity**

Rudolf Steiner reports that the various animal species were also created as beings existing outside of us, in order that true human beings would eventually emerge. This is because animals alter the reservoir of soul-forces which permeates the planet's aura, and which affects us, to some extent. Some animal species remove unpleasant forces from potentially coming into us, whilst other species bring about alterations in the Earth's energies which assist us to develop special features in our senses or cognition. But the theme of people killing animals, often for eating, brings up two associated thoughts: one is that the forces of animals which are consumed, in some way, may have an effect in the human being.

The second is, if an animal species is exterminated, then its group-soul has lost the ability to be present through having these animals on the Earth; and the loss of these animals is detrimental to the planet and to humanity, for various obvious reasons, and also because the existence of these animals alters the underlying matrix of the astral energies of the Earth's soul. This link that we have to all three primary animal species is also implicit in the south blue window, even though only the bird is depicted, as an archive document from Rudolf Steiner shows (see illustration 12).

We now cross over to explore the north Blue Window.

12 Right: A sketch by Rudolf Steiner, from the Archives. A document for the south Blue Window. Although the window only includes interaction with a bird and human being, this sketch shows that all three animal species are involved.

Left: Another archive document, for the Red Window. Several times on this sketch there are diagrams showing Saturn, sun and moon as forming a unified celestial body: the solar system.

The north Blue Window

Thinking

And he is seeing | *The world gives him sight* | *And he makes himself able to see*

THE NORTH BLUE WINDOW

Rudolf Steiner wrote this one word about the theme of this window
Thematic Overview: "Denken" = Thinking

The key features of the scenes
In the **left** panel: a human being is walking up a track, in a confused way. Above are two spirits, each holding an eye, and below are three geometrical shapes.

In the **central** panel: below are three divine beings from whose rays the fourfold life-forms on Earth have developed. Above these are three angels sounding trumpets, and above them three spheres, resounding.

In the **right** panel: the person is now walking along with a clear sight of where he or she is intending to go; near this person the sun is rising, and two angels each are holding an arm.

Important observation about this window's script: "THINKING"
When Rudolf Steiner used the word 'thinking', he often used it in a special way: in the sense of higher cognizing, or higher consciousness abilities. In other words, **seeing** with your soul and your spirit, which we normally refer to as clairvoyance, or spiritual seership. But in anthroposophy, these higher states of cognition are preceded by the ability to think clearly and intuitively about spiritual ideas. Also when a person is cognizing clairvoyantly, then they are indeed cognizing, and cognizing is the term for recognizing in your mind an idea or a mental picture, etc. So to call seership, 'thinking' is accurate, as clairvoyance cannot really be called feeling or willing. Consequently in Rudolf Steiner's view, 'thinking', was not restricted to logical thought, but it included cognising spiritual realities. There are three higher states of consciousness or seership.

Exploring the north Blue Window

Left Panel:

Keynote script: ***Und er sieht = And he is seeing***

When gazing at the windows, we keep in mind that the left panel shows the current situation which is often in need of improvement, or is the initial phase of process, whereas the right panel shows the next step, that is, the outcome (which is often an improved situation). In the left panel of the north blue window, we see an imperfect situation, as compared to the right panel. A person is walking along in an unsure way. His hand gesture is that of a troubled, uncertain person.[57] Up above, one Angel has an eye, and is near to the moon, the second Angel also has an eye and is placed near to the sun; and we note that the sun is not out-raying, but 'in-drawing'.

This 'in-drawing' feature indicates that here the sun is on the etheric level; it is not the physical sun, nor the divine (Devachanic) spiritual sun. This panel is telling us about how our eyes, which give us our physical vision, are formed not only from matter, but also by the action of etheric forces from the sun.[58] It is also telling us that one eye (on the right) is a solar-influenced eye; the other (on the left) is a lunar-influenced eye. We note too the prominence given to the sun, as it is in the highest place in the scene; this indicates that both eyes are created and maintained by the light-ether streaming out from the sun. Also the moon is shown as waxing, thus receiving ever more of the solar light, indicating that the lunar-influenced eye is nevertheless, formed from the sun's forces.

Below the person are three well-defined geometrical shapes, silhouetted against the dark earth. To understand the significance of these shapes is really important. They are not about crystalline

[57] The interpretation (G. Hartmann) that this gesture means, experiencing the cosmos in his thinking, is unconvincing.
[58] The interpretation (G. Hartmann) that these are 'eyes of the cosmos' appears unconvincing.

and organic (shapeless) earthly substances; but about the process of the human being bringing their soul-spirit nature into what they are doing. As we shall see with the central panel, the triangle represents the threefold mind, and the pentagram represents the Spiritual-self. We shall consider these further when we explore the right panel.

The central panel of the north Blue Window

Keynote script: ***Die Welt giebt ihn das Sehen = The world gives him seeing/sight***

We noted earlier that the over-script for this window is "Thinking", and that in Rudolf Steiner's world-view, it also refers to higher consciousness or clairvoyance, in the deeper sense. So again we can confirm that this window is about achieving higher cognition, or seership. The first stage of higher cognizing is called by Rudolf Steiner '*Imagination*', which refers to what we could call, '*psychic-image consciousness*', because it results in images being cognized, whether in the astral realm or in the ethers. (The use of the word *Imagination* in anthroposophy can be misleading, because in normal English it simply means 'fantasy'.) This panel presents an instructive view of what the person sees with their seership in the Soul-world. We could call this an 'instructive scene', rather than a more natural scene, because as seership develops, the seeker normally perceives the soul (or aura) of other beings, whether spirits or people.

So this Blue Window is about '*Imagination*' or seeing into the soul world (or the astral realm). But a primary dynamic of earthly life, when viewed from the astral world or soul realm, is depicted here: namely the fourfold principle that underlies life on Earth. So what is this central clairvoyant experience? What is the fourfold viewpoint it gives? A fourfold quality to life is presented in the famous vision of Ezekiel, the Hebrew seer, from the 6th century BC, who was living in Babylonia. He wrote about his vision of a spirit being with the faces of a human, lion, eagle and bull; and a similar theme also occurs in the Book of Revelation. These texts refer to an image with the three principle animal forms and the human being, this fourfold being is called the Tetramorph. The same perception is presented in this window; so let's explore what this is.

Firstly, we see here that four realities (or 'life-waves') are arising through the activity of three spiritual beings on the left side of the panel – namely, the eagle, the lion, the bull, and near to the bull, the human being: thus making four types of beings arise out of three creative forces.* The number three in regard to deity is often found in older spiritual philosophies. For example, in Hinduism, there is Brahma, Vishnu and Shiva; in ancient Sumeria there was Anu, Enlil and Ea, and in Christianity, the Holy Trinity. These all represent awareness of a threefold creative principle, or triune god, as originator of creation. In anthroposophical wisdom, the human being reflects its triune creator(s) through the threefold mind (thinking, feeling and will) and also through the three body systems (brain, heart-lungs and digestion). It is these three systems which allow the threefold mind to manifest.

Bull, Lion and Eagle

This panel is telling the viewer that the triune Creator is also reflected outside of us, in the existence of the animal life-waves; namely, bovine (bull), feline (lion) and avian (eagle). This panel is also pointing to the interconnectedness of the human being to the animal world. As Rudolf Steiner explained, the bovine animals in the world have an inner link to the human capacity for a digestion system, and hence indirectly to our limbs, which receive the energy they use from the digestive process. The lions embody energies which have an inner link to our heart, and hence to our feelings; and the eagle has a corresponding connection to the head (and hence our thinking).[59]

This panel is a contemplation on the inner link between the human being and the forces behind the three animal life-waves. There are, Rudolf Steiner taught, six or seven main animal groups, brought about by the planetary energies interacting with sun and moon forces as they permeated the Earth's aura. The vast number of different animal species living on the Earth, is based on these seven, plus variations produced by influences of the zodiac. The reason that it is these

[59] See his lecture cycle "Man as Symphony of the Creative Word" (GA 230).

three animal groups – bovine, feline and avian – which are portrayed in this window, is that these three are also a reflection of three of the four primary zodiacal energies: Taurus, Leo and Scorpio.

Inside the three energy-streams

There are small features inside the rays sent from the three spirit-beings from the sun across to the four life-forms on the Earth. Inside those rays from the spirit being whose energies stream out to the human being and to the bull, there are small spheres, like small moons. Inside the rays from the spirit being whose energies stream out to the bull and the lion, there are small stars. There are many small wave-forms in the rays from the spirit being whose energies stream out to the eagle and the lion. These three features are telling the viewer that the three kinds of spiritual energies involved here are quite different to each other. These differences of course refer to the different inner nature of the three creative beings forming our world and from whom the unique nature of the three main animal forces derive. It is very significant that these three streams of divine creativity are shown as coming from the sun, as we shall see.

But the central panel is especially pointing out the core truth that humanity is a fourth, emerging life-wave, arising from the integrating, and then overcoming of, the three principle animal qualities. In spiritual realms we have indeed a true spiritual essence, but on the Earth, the effort has to be made to overcome primordial animalistic tendencies. (See the small book, *The Two Gems of Rudolf Steiner*, for more about this.) This perspective on earthly existence is a modern re-statement of the ancient spiritual wisdom which created the mythical Sphinx, wherein a human head surmounts a body composed of a bull torso, eagle's wings and lion legs. In ancient times this full, fourfold sphinx was central in the Mysteries of Mesopotamia and Egypt.[60]

It is a primary element in the anthroposophical view of creation that the evolving of life on Earth is directed by divine beings, whose sphere of manifestation in our solar system, is the sun.* Furthermore, in an earlier phase of the current aeon, our Earth was cast out of the sun. So we owe our origin, in many respects, to the sun. The beings who brought forth the Earth, and guide its ongoing evolution, are called the 'sun-spirits'. Rudolf Steiner taught that these are the divine beings called, in the New Testament, the 'Powers', and these same divine beings are spoken of in the Book of Genesis, as creating the world. There they are referred to as the 'Elohim' in Hebrew, but translated simply as a single deity, 'God', in the Bible.

In this central panel, the three beings depict spirits who are a kind of group-soul for the three animal species relevant to humanity. But those particularly high spirits, the Powers, have been, and are still, sending forth their intentions as spiritual energies into the Earth-sphere, just as do the group-soul spirit beings. As a result of these combined influences, one portion of the four earthly types of living beings did gradually integrate the three main animal life-waves and thereby transcend them: humanity. That is, we human beings were able arise up out of the surrounding animalistic environment, and establish ourselves as a fully separate, fourth life-wave. As a result of this process, long ages ago, four basic types of human beings began to emerge. Three of these groups of human beings each still showed some likeness to one of the three animal types.

In this panel, some features of the human being depicted here point towards what arises when our normal earthly ego-sense is allowed to become spiritualized; for the face has three geometrical forms on its brow – a triangle, a pentagram and a hexagram. These symbols have to do with the uniquely human quality that distinguishes us from the animals, namely our 'ego' or a sense of self. But we bear in mind that our 'ego; or "I" is a combination of an earthly and a higher ego.* (See Part Two for more about this.)

Just above the four group-spirits, we see three Angels with trumpets resounding; they are 'speaking' to the four groups of living beings on the Earth. This is telling us how influential is the presence of the three divine spiritual forces, whose raying forth of energies created the threefold earthly reality. It is also the case that the seer in this experience becomes aware that the three

[60] The Egyptians never depicted this sphinx, however, Rudolf Steiner taught that they knew it very well.

primary animal life-waves do 'speak' to humanity. They have a message about life, especially about the interconnectedness of their reality with ours. *

On the top of the window there are three globes, and from these globes, tones are resounding. This appears to indicate the divine heavenly (or devachanic) threefold creator, and the three realms, from which the triune earthy reality was created. That there are three of these, contrasts with the four-fold structure below; and this 'four below, three above' pattern, correlates to the structure of the human being, which has the fourfold lower aspects, and the triune higher aspects. That is, the fourfold human being has a physical body, an etheric body, astral body and an earthly ego-sense: whereas above these, the human spirit is triune. In anthroposophy, these three spiritual elements are called the Spirit-self, the Life-spirit and the Spirit-human. (These are known in theosophical language as Manas, Buddhi and Atma.) The Spirit-self arises as the soul becomes spiritualised, and then the Life-spirit is formed as the life-forces, or etheric body, is spiritualized; and finally, when the hidden divine will-energies within the physical body are released, then the mysterious 'Spirit-human' arises. *

A comment by Rudolf Steiner implies that what this central panel portrays was experienced "wherever initiation into the astral realm occurred".[61] Here I can provide some evidence for just how uniform and wide-spread was the experience being revealed in this window for a person being initiated in ancient times. Early in the 20th century a number of scrolls were discovered, from the 4th century AD, written by a group of remote Chinese Buddhists, living on the edge of the Gobi Desert. These people had the good fortune to be taught by some spiritual teachers belonging to the movement, which began in Persia, known as the 'Manicheans'.

This means that these Chinese people absorbed a profound, esoteric Christianity. We cannot go into the details of this group here, but in essence the Manicheans were following the deeply esoteric teachings of a great teacher called Mani or Manes, born AD 276 in Persia. This initiate taught an esoteric, cosmic Christianity, which teaches that the cosmic sun god 'Christ', was distinct from the man Jesus. This view, that these two became eternally united, spiritually, in the Baptism in the Jordan and especially through the Resurrection events, is also part of anthroposophical wisdom. (We shall return to this theme later.)

This cosmic Christianity was so cosmopolitan and so inspiring, that there were people in all spiritual-religious groups across much of the northern hemisphere, who became 'Manicheans'. Included in the literature of the remote Chinese community was a series of hymns of praise to Jesus. A passage from one of the Chinese scrolls, written in an ancient dialect, is startling to read, once you know about this Blue Window. Here is an extract from one of their hymns to Jesus,

> Praise to Jesus:
> I thank thee, that Thou hast now opened the eyes of my Buddha-nature
> so that I may behold the four, tranquil wonderful Law-Bodies.
> Also I thank Thee, that Thou has opened the ears of my Buddha-nature
> so that I may hear the pure tones of the three Unchanging-Perpetuals.[62]

The expression "my Buddha-nature" can be understood as referring to the higher self, in particular the Spirit-self, with some of the Life-spirit present as well. The four "Law-Bodies" we can understand as the four dynamics and associated bodily forms that underlie the fourfold world of humans, birds, felines and bovines. The "Unchanging-Perpetuals" we can understand as referring to the threefold creative power that has brought our world into being.

Sun and Moon - Space and Time

In this panel, low down, are the sun and the moon, these are portrayed from a physical world perspective, not from within the etheric or astral reams. Here the stars around the sun and moon are grouped in two different ways. One group is somewhat circular, the other more linear. To most people the sun has a natural association with linear space, because in our minds, the

---

[61] GA 104a, lect. 11th May 1909, *The Imagery of the Apocalypse of St. John.*

[62] I am indebted to Professor Helwig Schmidt-Glinzter for sharing with me his specialist translation work on the scrolls, now in Beijing, written in an archaic Chinese dialect.

universe extends far out into space. In contrast to the sun, the moon with its cycles of 28 and 29.5 days and its 18.6 year nodal cycle, is associated naturally with the flow of time. We are accustomed to think of the moon as a timekeeper that regularly goes through its cycles, in a cyclical way.* The association here of the sun with space also points to a deep element of anthroposophical cosmology. This is, that space itself came into being as a result of the sun emerging from the vast field of consciousness and energies which was the diffuse, primeval solar system – in a remote Age, which we can call the Sun Aeon.[63]

The reason that the perspective here on the sun and the moon is a physical one, is that this scene wants to point our attention to the creating and ongoing nurturing of the three primary animal life-waves and of humanity, in our solar system. So, having the sun and moon below is a guide to contemplating how the interaction, brought about by spirit beings, between sun, moon and the Earth, in the world of space and time, has resulted in what our physical life here on the Earth now has within it.

The sun and moon are also shown above, but less clearly. * On the left this time is the sun, and its link to lineal space is pointed out by the long thin bar just underneath it. The moon is now on the right, as a crescent, but it is also shown as the full moon together with various crescents. They are each placed just below the Angels with trumpets; and each has its association with the physical world of time and space. In this position they remain a pointer to this same dynamic, about space and time; but their positions are reversed. Rudolf Steiner taught that in the astral world, physical things are seen reversed; thus a number such as '234' seen in an astral vision, actually refers to '432' in our world. That the moon and sun are reversed, seems to point to the dynamic that the spatial solar system is still the context here, but now the focus is on influences impacting on the physical world that we live in, but emanating from the astral realm. For in the astral realm, things can be reversed to what we experience in the physical world.

The right panel of the north Blue Window

Keynote script: ***Und er macht sich sehend* = *And he makes himself able to see***

In this panel, the message is about achieving seership, or higher thinking. So, the person is now walking along under a waning moon, towards a powerful, large sun which is not so distant, and which is actually the spiritual sun, for the rays from it are dark; this suggests non-physical light. So here the person has developed higher consciousness, or powers of seership, and is able to direct her or his steps towards the spiritual sun. The two spirit beings are now holding an arm each, which appears to me to refer to the will of the human person, since our limbs are the organs of the will.

Silhouetted against the dark earth are those three shapes from the left panel, but they have lost their geometrical quality, and are now rather shapeless. We noted earlier that the triangle represents the soul, and the pentagram represents the Spiritual-self. There is also a seven-pointed shape, which appears to represent the soul – as a product of the solar system, the seven planets.[64] To understand this feature, we need to really grasp the message of this window; namely that the acolyte is striving towards seership in the sense of higher consciousness. Thus in the left panel, the person's body language, with the hand to their forehead, shows uncertainty; or, in terms of the much sought-after goal of higher initiatory consciousness, it shows inner confusion. In other words, such a person is physically seeing, but not yet spiritually. The soul and (germinal) spiritual capacities have not been brought into effective action; these have not permeated the person, living as they are in their physical life and body. The geometrical forms represent the soul-spirit capacities of the human being which have not as yet been incorporated into their earthly consciousness.

Now in this right panel, the person has achieved seership, and as a consequence the soul-spirit part of the human being has been brought into effective action. So, despite the obstacles of the

[63] GA 132, lect. 7th Nov. 1911.

[64] There are few uses by Steiner of a seven-pointed shape (e.g., GA 104a, p.20), but it is a very uniform star in the context of a cosmic deity.

consciousness being immersed in a physical body, seership has been attained. And here in the right panel, these forms are now shapeless. I have concluded that this indicates that the spiritual capacities of the person have been brought down into the physical world – that is, they are integrated into their consciousness in the physical body. That is why they are shapeless. Why would the loss of geometrical shape indicate this? Firstly, if we consider those shapes in the left panel, we see that they are still geometrical, but we also noted that the person has not, as yet, found a way forwards spiritually. But in the right panel, progress has been made, and these spiritual abilities are now developed. So the spiritual abilities have been empowered, and incorporated into their personality. But this also implies that the soul-spirit nature has been integrated into the physical, bodily existence, which is here symbolically expressed as losing their geometrical shaping.

Such a dynamic is similar to what happens to the soul prior to birth. Rudolf Steiner has described how the soul of a person who is waiting to be born, and hovering above their mother, has a number of specific forms in his or her aura, which reflect the structure of the cosmos. He describes how the soul of the person rays its forces down into the embryo, forming the internal organs of its future body. He comments that as the internal organs gain their structure and shape, these fine geometrical forms in the aura lose their symmetrical shape,

> ...in this process, the astral becomes more and more shapeless {in respect of its internal structure}, because it has been sending its {own} specific forms, which it brought with it from another phase of its existence {in the cosmos} down into the body's physical organs....thus does the astral body become more or less simply cloud-shaped.[65]

Secondly, Rudolf Steiner has commented on a related topic. For an initiate or highly evolved soul, as they seek re-birth, which means bringing the higher soul-spirit capacities into their incarnate consciousness, is not easy; it is not an 'automatic' process, and can be very difficult. He spoke for example about, the Italian political-social reformer, Garabaldi, who only carried out ineffectual political actions in the mid-nineteenth century. This was because although he was an initiate in an earlier life, he was unable to be truly or fully himself. He was unable to manifest his high spiritual capacities, because of the obstacles that his body created. But here in the right panel, these forms, now shapeless, indicates that this person has awakened their spiritual abilities, bringing about seership; and this meant bringing their spiritual energies into the reality of their incarnate, physical life. We shall see a clearer example of this same dynamic in the south Purple Window.[66]

NORTH BLUE WINDOW: PART TWO

* The group spirits on the sun

A deeper message in this panel refers to the long past evolutionary journey of humanity. It was this process of the sun and the Earth separating, long ages ago, which allowed those spirit-beings who are closely linked to the fourfold life-wave that we now have on our Earth – the bovine, the feline, the birds and the human beings – to evolve to higher, non-material states of being. They were no longer so closely linked to their more earthly creatures. These beings are like 'group-souls' of the four life-waves existing on the Earth, and when the separation of sun and planet occurred, they continued their activity from the sun as guiding, helping beings for these four groups. It was in the Atlantean Age that there emerged the four distinct types of human beings which we briefly noted earlier. Three of the human groups each had some resemblance to one of the three animal types; but the fourth group developed ever more a distinctly human character.

However, on the planet now orbiting as a satellite around the sun, a polar opposite process occurred: this earthly world with its four groups, could now become ever more dense. Over millions of years it gradually became the dense, hardened world we have today.[67] During this

[65] GA 212, p. 119, lecture, 26 May 1922.
[66] Schmelzer's view of this panel: a more will-focussed orientation to the world....which enables the person to comprehend a more advanced natural phenomenon than {merely} the crystalline shapes, of the left panel, namely organic {shapeless} forms, is unconvincing.
[67] GA 112, 25th June 1909, *The Gospel of St. John.*

same time, on the sun, the most evolved of these group-soul spirits further developed themselves, and together with spiritual influences from the great sun gods, became the archetypes of humanity, of the human life-wave. Through the influences from the archetypal inspiring spirits of a true humanity, the existence of this fourth group was fully established. But the activity of these 'archetypal' spirits, in regard to the individualizing human beings, was assisted through the influence of especially high spirit beings: the great sun-spirits or Powers.

Their influence means that as humanity consolidated into a life-wave, each person would have the potential to arise to the true ego: to their threefold spirit. The earlier initiates contemplated this great drama of evolution through the image of the Sphinx. In this perspective, the bull represents the physical body, the lion represents the etheric body, the eagle represents the soul, and of course the human being depicts the normal earthly person, or one could say, the ego-sense.

*** The bull near to the human**
In the depictions of the four beings, the bull and the human being are placed nearer to each other. This is because the bull represents the dense physical state of being, and it is through the dense, physical bodily condition that the human being achieves its earthly ego-sense. It is also an indicator that it is in the fourth aeon that this denser material state came about; this aeon (the Earth aeon) is governed by Taurus. A central star-group in Taurus are the Pleiades, and these are a very prominent, very revered, star-group in the star-lore of many ancient cultures, showing an awareness of the central role of Taurus in this current evolutionary age.

*** The higher ego**
The human face in the central panel is rather blank, with closed eyes. This is because the earthly ego is in many ways, illusory. But on the forehead are those symbols we have noted. The triangle refers to the soul, with its three main qualities of thinking, feeling and will. The pentagram is a symbol of the next level in our nature, our Spirit-self; the hexagram is used by Rudolf Steiner to symbolise an even higher aspect of the human spirit, the Life-Spirit. The Life-Spirit is only present in a germinal form in humanity, but it arises when the soul has developed the Spiritual-self, and can then spiritualize its etheric energies. This person then has healing powers and intense creative powers that can, at times, bring about miracles. The following verse from Rudolf Steiner can serve as a contemplation on this deep mystery, of the earthly person as a mirror of their higher ego,

In human hearts there beats
the highest forces of the Earth,
Within the human being
live the Powers of the Soul-realm.
To human striving there beckons
the goals of Spirit-land.
However the human "I" itself
is spirit in Spirit-expanses.
And what in the human being
calls itself "I"
is only a mirror
of the truth of its own Self.[68]

Also, part of a verse from Rudolf Steiner's Soul Calendar (verse 6) illustrates the underlying message of this scene in the central panel,

The world – as divine archetype –
everywhere shows to me
the truth of my own image.

[68] Published in GA 40 p. 214.

*** The Angels with trumpets**
There is a deeper meaning to these Angels with their resounding trumpets. Notice how two of them are directing their sounds towards the moon, which now, for this purpose, represent the night-time. During the Atlantean Age, which is the epoch that occurred before the Great Flood, each of these four groups of human beings had their distinctive appearance, either a (primitive) human appearance or people with somewhat lion-like, bull-like or eagle-like features. In anthroposophical wisdom, the time we have whilst asleep, and thus immersed in spiritual realms, is considered important. In regard to this, Rudolf Steiner taught that in the Atlantean Age, these four groups of human beings whilst asleep, were all exposed to the resonance, or the resounding 'calls' of their respective archetypal group-spirit. He explained that these tones reinforced their inner sense of what kind of human being they were.[69]

*** The interconnectedness of the animal reality with ours**
The bull forces still exist within the astral body of the man, and the lion forces still exist within the etheric body of the woman; these are negative influences, contributing to the lower-self. And indeed, Rudolf Steiner taught that the etheric body of both man and woman contains, weakly, the entire tapestry of all animal species, and these could all appear as a great tapestry around a person when their etheric body is released from the physical body. But he emphasizes, this does not happen because of the active presence in our etheric body of influences from divine beings: namely the Angels, Archangels and the Principalities.[70]

*** The sun and moon in physical and astral realms**
We also need to note here that in the nine windows, there are two ways of depicting the influence of the sun and the moon. This is either as experienced in the astral realm, or as seen in the physical world. In the Red Window, and as we shall discover, also in the south Pink Window, the sun and the moon are depicted from an astral perspective. On the astral level, the moon has lineal or straight rays from it; whilst the sun has circular energies spreading from it. But in the blue window, they are depicted from the physical world viewpoint. So, here the moon has curved or circular features, whilst the sun has linear features.

As we noted earlier, the position of the two bodies is reversed where they are depicted above the three divine beings, this is pointing to their significance in our physical world, but experienced from within the astral world. So the sun and moon in this part of the window which closely linked to the Angels with trumpets, is telling us that in our solar system, above space and time, on the astral level, the Word is resonating ! That is, as we noted earlier, the influences of the three divine beings is resonating across from the sun to the Earth and moon.

So the depiction of sun and moon **below** the three divine beings and their creations, is about experiencing the interdependence of humanity and animals within us. Whilst the depiction of sun and moon **above** the divine beings is about experiencing the interdependence of humanity and animals outside of us, in the cosmos. Here are the two great pathways that characterized the ancient Mysteries: the Path Within and the Path Without. These terms refer to the spiritual influences within the microcosm, and the spiritual influences up in the macrocosm.

We now walk over to our right to explore the South Purple Window.

---

[69] GA 104, 22nd June 1908, *The Apocalypse of St. John.*
[70] Archive lecture: 20th Mar. 1916. (Published 7th Jan 1940, in *Das Goetheanum Wochenschrift.*)

The south Purple Window

It will be *It comes into being* *It is*

THE SOUTH PURPLE WINDOW

Colour Overview

We need to be clear about what colour the next two windows are, because there is often a misunderstanding about 'purple' and 'violet', especially when the German text is translated into English (and other languages). As I wrote in the *Rudolf Steiner Handbook*;

> Wherever you read the term 'violet' in English, in anthroposophical books, **what is actually meant is purple.**[71] This is because in German the word for 'purple' is borrowed from the French language, namely 'violette'. And this is often incorrectly understood to mean 'violet' to translators. When red and blue are mixed in equal parts, purple arises; but if there is more blue then violet forms. If there is more red added, then magenta or cerise is formed.[72]

So the next windows are purple, not violet (even though the slides for sale of these two windows make them appear violet). Here are some brief comments from Rudolf Steiner about the nature of purple,

> Purple in the aura of the soul, shows piety and religious fervour....I affirm life and my existence, from a spiritual perspective......whereas in the aura of the Spirit, this colour shows service to the world, and a will to be self-sacrificing... it shows that the person is accustomed to immersion in prayer.[73]
>
> And also, he taught that it speaks of 'the soul arising within the spiritual' (Im Geiste sich erstehende Seelische). [74]

Thematic Overview:
There is no over-script from Rudolf Steiner, but this window is obviously about the process of descending down to a new life on Earth.

A brief overview features of the scenes
In the **left** panel: a young person close to the earth and near to the moon, above are two spirit being, on either side of a sphere.

In the **central** panel: below, we see a future mother and father to whom spiritual forces are descending; above there is a Janus-headed entity, near to a small group of people, also some plants and three bright forms.

In the **right** panel: a child is being lowered down towards the moon, and thus the Earth, by two spirit beings.

Exploring the south Purple Window

Left Panel:

Keynote script: ***Es wird sein*** = ***It will be***

In this left panel, we see a child on the Earth, being watched by two spirit beings from high above. The bright sphere near these two beings, very likely is the sun, and hence it appears that these beings are from the sun sphere. Rudolf Steiner has explained that on the way down to a new life, it is in the sun sphere that the new personality is formed, and once this happens, then the

---

[71] In books of lectures by Rudolf Steiner, and in other books, for example, of Liane Colot D'Herbois, and Hilde Raske's book, *The Language of Colour*, the term 'violet' is almost always wrong and should read 'purple'.
[72] Hence there are three nuances of lilac. Pale purple produces lilac, but pale violet produces bluish lilac and pale magenta produces pinkish lilac.
[73] GA 9, p. 252.
[74] GA 291a, p.321.

journey down to the Earth is inevitable. We shall explore the reason for the child being near to the moon, when we look at the right panel. In the earth area, below the child, we see the same three geometrical forms that we saw in the north Blue Window. We shall consider these too, when we explore the right panel.

Two spirit-beings in the sun sphere gaze down at the soul which is on its way down towards conception. Consequently the moon is shown as waxing; so its influence is getting stronger in regard to the soul on its way down to a new life. And, as in the north Blue Window, the spiritual qualities of the human being are free: that is, they are not yet functioning within the consciousness of a person who is embodied, or immersed in the physical-etheric body.

The central panel of the south Purple Window

Keynote script: ***Es entsteht*** = ***It comes into being***

This window is about the mysterious process whereby we become incarnated, which means enwrapped in a physical body. Many people have had an experience about what happens after death; however it is very rare to find a source of knowledge about the process that brings a soul down to birth, but Rudolf Steiner had the ability to research this elusive theme.

We see at the top of the panel, a two-faced or 'Janus' figure which has some plant forms near it. And, higher up to the left are several people, whilst on the right, our attention is drawn down towards some descending forms, which go further down towards the parents. To understand this feature, we need to know that the soul, as it descends to the Earth for a new life, is in the soul world, until it draws quite near to the Earth and enters the moon sphere, and is then within the ethers surrounding the Earth. At this point in its journey, its new life-force body or 'etheric body' is formed, which connects the soul to the (future) physical body. Since plants are a symbol of the etheric forces, this two-faced figure represents the boundary between the soul world and the etheric realm. On its left, the soul is saying farewell to friends, just above the border of the lunar sphere, where this person shall soon encounter the etheric energies. So the viewpoint here is dualistic, looking back to the cosmos out of which one has descended, and also down towards the Earth.

The scenes below this are not in real time, nor are they fully 'naturalistic', but they present the essence of the process. Above the father-to-be, a long, darkish comet-shaped form is descending. This is the germinal essence of the new physical body for the incarnating child. This germinal essence is formed by the child's spirit up in the divine realms, and is the expression of the deeper layers of the will of the person incarnating. This will-force determines the unique nature of the body, and has zodiacal forces within it. This germinal essence exists in the father's etheric body, and can imprint itself upon the embryo from the moment of conception. In many cases, but not all, it has been incorporated into the father's male ancestry, some centuries ago.

Extending up above the aura of the mother-to-be, several layers of spiritual energies are depicted. Above these, to the left, three shapes are to be seen, and they are beginning to be drawn gradually downwards, in thin streams, towards the woman. These represent the three soul qualities of the incarnating child (thinking, feeling and willing) which shall gradually become somewhat entwined with the aura of the mother. This soul en-sheathing shall remain with the child until it reaches its adolescence. (It is significant that in the horoscope of a child, there are often some **core** features which are similar to the mother's.) Once the person is born, then the physical sunshine lights up their world, and in like measure, the spiritual light becomes veiled.

The right panel of the south Purple Window

Keynote script: ***Es ist*** = ***It is***

In this panel the process of becoming conceived is now about to happen, and so two spirit beings are depicted as lowering the human being down into readiness for conception. Hence the moon is shown here as artificially inverted, with echoes going earthwards, as if to say, "into the Moon sphere you go".

We see here that the three geometrical forms are depicted twice: up above in the air and down below. In the air below the moon, they are still well-formed, and this is similar to what we see in the left panel. Earlier, we saw these forms in the north Blue Window, and it was my conclusion then, that when these forms become shapeless, this indicated that the spiritual capacities of the person have been brought down into the physical world – that is, they are integrated into their consciousness in the physical body. In the Blue Window, it was a matter of the meditating person applying himself or herself to the accessing higher consciousness as an earthly person. Here it is quite a different theme: the process of becoming incarnate. But a similar dynamic applies here. In the left panel, the person is not yet incarnate, they are waiting for this to happen, so the three shapes are still geometrical, as the soul-spirit of the human being is not immersed in matter.

But in the right panel this dynamic – of a person's soul-spirit existing either within, or not within, the physical realm – is being especially emphasized. At first, where the soul is about to begin the process of incarnating, these shapes, up in the air, are still geometrical. But the second depiction shows them as being within the earthly sphere, where they are now shapeless: this change appears to indicate that the conception process has now occurred. The person's body has just been conceived, so these starry forms lose their well-defined shapes. In connection with this, the second crescent moon, facing downwards, appears to emphasize the dominating power that the moon has, once a person's body is conceived. The three shapeless forms appear as if held by lunar energies, which is appropriate, because the moon governs the ether forces. So once the embryo begins to develop, the moon has a prominent influence. The process of gestation draws on the ether forces of the child and of the mother, and these are very much governed by the moon.

Of the two spirit-beings shown here, one is probably a Principality (or Archai, in Greek); these beings have a task to do with ensuring that the correct family is chosen. And the other being is probably an Archangel, for it is these beings who determine into which nation or folk a person incarnates, and they also assist in regard to the forming of the etheric body.

We now walk to our right, across the hall to explore the North Purple Window.

The north Purple Window

It had become *It has been* *It was*

NORTH PURPLE WINDOW

Thematic Overview
There is no over-script from Rudolf Steiner for this window, but its theme is obviously about leaving this world, just as its opposite, in the south wall, is about coming into the world.

Brief overview of the three panels
Left panel: a spirit-being is taking a human being up and away from their embodied state.

Central panel: someone is dying on a bed, and their life is depicted along a spiral path, going backwards in time, back to their infancy. Above are various features including three bright forms and an eye in a triangle.

Right panel: a lion is poised, ready for action; above it, there is a human being who is enclosed in a shelter, while higher up two spirit-beings are depicted.

EXPLORING THE NORTH PURPLE WINDOW

Left Panel:

Keynote script: ***Es war geworden* = *It had become***

This panel depicts in a symbolic way, the process of dying – as experienced from the spiritual realms, and in particular from the viewpoint of one's own Guiding Angel. (As we shall see, the central panel depicts the same process, but from within the human being's consciousness.) The Angel is assisting the human being to exit from their flesh body, represented by the skeleton, which across the ages has been a representation of death.* Above the skeleton is a face, representing the etheric body, which has a similar form to the physical body. This life-force organism gradually dissolves into the world's ethers, or 'the cosmic ether' as Rudolf Steiner calls it. (In his teachings on this subject the reader will find a wealth of detail and many invaluable insights, unique in literature, about this process.)[75]

Above the face is a triangle, representing the threefold soul, or 'astral body', and above this is a star, which represents the human spirit. Behind and above all of this, is a general impression of brightness. This appears to indicate the shining radiance of the astral realm, which is a feature of near-death-experiences. This is a radiance which appears in stark contrast to the physical sunlight that the soul was exposed to, (or restricted to) whilst in a body. In the lower part of the panel, a very striking feature is to be seen. A bovine form (that is, a cow or bull) is magically emerging out of the mysterious background.

Moreover, the gesture of this image here is saying that this bovine is experiencing itself as having just been released, and it is thus springing forth, to disappear far away into the astral aura of the Earth. What does this feature mean? It refers to the role of astral forces linked to the bovine species, in the creating and maintaining of our physical, flesh body. This takes us back to the theme of those three primary animal energies which were so prominent in the north blue window.

The spiritual archetype or group-soul of the bovines has been created in part by spiritual energies from Taurus. These animals especially bring about a 'Taurean' influence in the world, which is responsible for the over-all dense nature of matter, in this case, of our physical body. When a person dies, this dense earthy quality, permeating the physical body, is no longer needed, and so it is no longer bound to the body. Awareness of this profound secret existed long ago in the ancient Egyptian Mysteries, as is revealed in tomb paintings from this culture about what the person experiences as they die. These have very similar depictions to this window; the front part of a bovine entity (called Hathor) is simply emerging out of the background, in the realm of the

[75] For example, in his book *Theosophy*, and *Life between Death and Rebirth*.

16 The bovine forces emerging at death — ancient Egyptian artwork for the after-life.
Hathor emerges straight out of the earth, from the west bank of the Nile, which means the realm of the Dead, when a person dies.
Left: from the Papyrus of Ani Wallis, edit. E.A. Wallis-Budge.
Right: from the tomb of Nesykhonsu 2051-2030 BC 21-22 Dynasty.

after-life. See two examples of this in illustration 16. In ancient Egypt, the west bank of the Nile represented the astral realm, or the soul world, where the soul goes when the body dies. One of these paintings is on a wooden coffin lid, from the late 21st to early 22nd dynasty, from the tomb of Nesykhonsu, depicting her making gold offerings to Hathor, who is emerging from the hillside, in western Thebes.

The central panel of the north Purple Window

Keynote script: ***Es ist gewesen*** = ***It has been***

Birth and death are the two most pivotal facts of human life; for birth gives access to the physical world, and thus to an experience of the sense of self, even if, esoterically viewed this ego-sense is partially illusory. Birth also gives the opportunity to encounter the lower-self, and the unique possibility to seek to overcome it. Death is the outcome of being born, and gives the soul and one's spiritual nature an opportunity to assimilate the experiences of life and to prepare for another, later incarnation. Hence, in Rudolf Steiner words,

> These two purple windows are closely linked. To esoteric consciousness, birth and death are not seen as separate phenomena.[76]

Here we see a dying human being; the spiral above them indicates that they are seeing their life's journey in a reverse sequence, from old age back to infancy. Let's explore all the features in this panel.

Mourners

Some shrouded figures can be seen near the death-bed. These figures, as originally drawn by Rudolf Steiner, are somewhat imprecise in their outlines, so it is possible that these may not only be living friends who are mourning the dying person, but may well include, or want to point towards, souls of people who died some time ago, and who have gathered around to greet their beloved friend, once he or she has fully left their body.

The Stars

The curving life-path shows, as Rudolf Steiner pointed out in a lecture, an aged person, then a couple in mid-life, then a child and finally a baby in a cradle. Near the child, four stars are shown. The stars refer to a spiritual aspect of childhood, which is the core principle of Steiner education; a child's intense imagination is due to their condition of not being fully immersed in their body. This means that they are open to influences from the higher worlds: that is, imaginative impressions living in the aura, flowing from the realms beyond the physical world, are present in the child's soul or aura.

This dynamic, of being open to imaginative impressions from higher realms, is represented by these stars. These stars also indicate the situation that throughout the child's etheric body, until the age of seven, there are many sparkling starry forms, reflecting the influence of stars and planets in their soul.[77]

The great poet and thinker, William Wordsworth, expressed awareness of this close link of the child's consciousness to the spiritual, in an imaginative way, in his poem, *Ode to immortality,*

> .....
> Our birth is but a sleep and a forgetting;
> the soul that rises with us, our life's Star
> hath had elsewhere its setting,
> and cometh from afar.
> Not in entire forgetfulness,

[76] GA 243 p. 214.
[77] GA 212, lecture, 26th May 1922.

nor in utter nakedness
but trailing clouds of glory do we come
from God, who is our home.
Heaven lies about us in our infancy !
Shades of the prison-house begin to close upon the growing boy... *

Three long shapes
Above the baby in the crib, there are three elongated forms, which come from a radiant light, which has concentric rings. It appears likely that these three forms refer to the last stage of the reversed view of one's journey through life. This takes the person back prior to conception, when from the threefold human spirit, and from the threefold higher heavenly realms (higher Devachan) the soul descended towards rebirth. These same forms also point to the return of the human spirit to the three higher realms of Heaven (or Devachan), which can be called the realm of God. In the original sketch from Rudolf Steiner, and thus in the first Goetheanum, two of these three forms are conjoined; but this feature was omitted in this window of the second Goetheanum. That two of these forms are conjoined, probably points to the structure of the triune human spirit; for the Spirit-self and the Life-Spirit share the one spiritual (devachanic) aura, whilst the Spirit-human aspect of our spirit (also called the Atma) has its own sublime aura. This conjoining could also point to the higher astral realm as one main realm into which the departing soul enters at first, and then the twofold Devachanic realm (lower and higher Devachan) which it enters later on.

The eye in a triangle
An eye by itself is a very old esoteric symbol, used long ago in ancient Egypt, and in various mystical groups in post-Renaissance Europe including Freemasonry, as a symbol of God. Rudolf Steiner has used it here, inside a triangle, to specifically represent the three qualities or strands of the human spirit: that is the Spirit-self, the Life-Spirit and the Spirit-human. So here it seems to point to the divine source of the human spirit to which the person who has died is returning. In traditional language, it is saying that 'the soul will return to God'. It also may be saying, that the after-life journey will take place according to the 'laws' that govern the way the spiritual realms receive into themselves a returning human soul and human spirit.

The three crosses
Now there are two other features to this scene: the Ten Commandments, and on the other side of the spiral, the crucifixion event on Golgotha hill. We shall consider this latter feature first. As the reader will have noticed already, the scenes in these windows touch on many deep themes, but my commentary is avoiding lengthy explanations. However, with the subject of Christianity, we touch on a theme which in anthroposophical wisdom is respected for its sacred nature, and about which Rudolf Steiner brought many radically new and profoundly sacred insights. An entire chapter in the *Rudolf Steiner Handbook* is dedicated to this theme, where I have presented my translations of various ancient Greek texts that illumine Rudolf Steiner's teachings on this theme. A good introduction to Rudolf Steiner's teachings on this subject is found in his book, *Christianity as Mystical Fact.* And, as I wrote in the *Rudolf Steiner Handbook,* "....a good place to start with his teachings on Christianity is his statement which has the quality of a Zen Buddhist koan, "Christianity began as a religion, but is greater than all religions, including Christianity."

In other words, what we understand Christianity to be, is something else; it is a reality which transcends the formal structure of a religion. Rudolf Steiner's perspective here is that the Christian scriptures present a sacred narrative, but they also veil a profound cosmic event, the understanding of which requires initiation wisdom. Once this deeper message is understood, these texts can become a source of real spiritual inspiration, because a deeply sacred, esoteric reality is discovered. To find these special truths one needs a feeling for the underlying esoteric worldview of the gospel writers. The Greek texts of the New Testament will be briefly referred to, here in my translations, where it helps to build a pathway to understanding Steiner's research.

Rudolf Steiner taught that underlying the Christian Scriptures is a veiled, cosmic viewpoint which sees humanity evolving on planet Earth in a series of Ages or time-cycles, during which humanity descends down from non-material realms into the physical, material Earth through many lifetimes. Then we gradually arise back into these spiritual realms. When Steiner's perspective on the Gospels is studied, these terms take on new meaning. The essential message of his esoteric Christianity is that the death and resurrection of Jesus Christ on Golgotha hill in Palestine, are events which have a pivotal role in this vast process whereby the human life-wave is given the opportunity to achieve its wonderful future goal.

You will probably be familiar with the phrase, "the kingdom of Heaven"; there is in fact no such phrase in the Greek text of the New Testament. Jesus never used it; he always says, "the kingdom of **the Heavens**". However, traditionally the translations always make it singular: (In Greek, *he basileia ton ouranon* ἡ βασιλεία τῶν οὐρανῶν). This 'flattening-out' occurs because historically in Christian theology, references to esoteric truths were unwelcome. The removal of the plural 'heavens' here, is done because it is assumed that a multiplicity of heavens is 'a superstitious idea', which Jesus made use of in a kindly way, in order to 'speak the language of the people'. But such an explanation of the text is both shallow and prejudiced.

In anthroposophy, the term 'Christ' refers to the cosmic being who came upon (or, 'anointed') Jesus at the Baptism in the Jordan River. So in anthroposophy, the person known as 'Jesus Christ' is a being consisting of the man Jesus, and also of the deity, the Christ being, who became present in him, as from the Baptism. This viewpoint of two distinct, but deeply interlinked, entities, who at the Resurrection formed together the divine 'god-man', was held as a sacred truth by some Christians in the early church, but later on, in less enlightened times, this was condemned as a heresy.

The positioning of the three crosses here near to the infant, has many meanings. It refers to the new opportunity given to human beings, by the Christ-event, who seek to undertake spiritual development, through their life of Earth. The spiritual light that now pervades the Earth's aura, ever since the Resurrection, has made accessible the source of the 'divine' within the human being; from this light that Spiritual-self is formed. The three crosses may also point to the teachings of Rudolf Steiner which confirm the ancient gospel teachings, that a pathway for the deceased person up through the astral realms, into its higher spheres, has been made possible through the Golgotha events. For the spiritual light which is accessible to the seeker after spirituality today, also illumines the after-life for those who have died.

The significance of the events of the Crucifixion and the Resurrection are enormous, as described in Rudolf Steiner's spiritual-scientific research into the significance of the union of the great sun god to the Earth's aura. Another reason then for the three crosses being placed here is to indicate the role of Christ in the after-death process, with respect, for example to the working of karma. The 'Grace' of Christ is an expression that is relevant here, because it refers to the providing of help to humanity in the battle against the lower-self and against malignant influences from Lucifer and Ahriman. The assistance given to humanity is a very large subject, but briefly put, it includes permeating the Earth with a source of spiritual light, from which the Spiritual-self, and also the Life-Spirit, can gradually be formed. The reader can study this theme in various works of Rudolf Steiner. The Golgotha events enable the state of one's soul, as one leaves the Earth, to be superior to what it was when one came into the world. It also includes opening the possibility to moderate the stern requirements of the law of karma; where a person can seek to invoke ethical insights into those who have hurt her or him, rather than to seek revenge.

The Ten Commandments

Now we need to explore the intriguing depiction of the Ten Commandments in this central panel. Firstly, we need to note that they are placed in two stone tablets, but in such a way that the first three are separated out from the remaining seven, even though there is room on the first tablet for more writing. This is done to emphasize a qualitative difference between the two groups. So what is the difference between Commandments 1-3 and Commandments 4-10? To understand this, we need, even if only briefly, to make ourselves familiar with the Commandments, and then with the immensely important perspective that Rudolf Steiner unveils about the Commandments and the mission of Moses **in regard to our sense of our own sense of self** (or ego-sense).

The Ten Commandments were, of course, given to the Israelites by Moses, in the 14th century BC. It is an old tradition that Moses has a connection to what people experience after they leave their physical body and awaken in the Soul-world. Rudolf Steiner taught in regard to Moses, that his mission was to bring about an awareness that the human being could start to consider their own self, and become aware that there is a potential higher, divine ego or Self, awaiting development in the human being.

Rudolf Steiner has divided the Ten Commandments into the first group which are about the command to sense and make alive in oneself, the divine self, whilst the other seven are grouped into a second category. But to do this, he had to actually number the Commandments in a different way to that done in the Bible. We know this from a lecture he gave on this topic. So first, let's see the Commandments as they appear usually in a Bible:

THE 10 COMMANDMENTS: From Exodus 20 and Deut 5: 6-21.

ONE
"You shall have no other gods before me.
TWO
"You shall not make for yourself an idol in the form of anything in heaven above or on the earth beneath, or in the waters below. You shall not bow down to them or worship them; for I, the LORD your God, am a jealous God, punishing the children for the sin of the fathers to the third and fourth generation of those who hate me, but showing love to a thousand generations of those who love me and keep my commandments.
THREE
"You shall not misuse the name of the LORD your God, for the LORD will not hold anyone guiltless who misuses his name.
FOUR
"Remember the Sabbath day by keeping it holy. Six days you shall labor and do all your work, but the seventh day is a Sabbath to the LORD your God. On it you shall not do any work, neither you, nor your son or daughter, nor your manservant or maidservant, nor your animals, nor the alien within your gates. For in six days the LORD made the heavens and the earth, the sea, and all that is in them, but he rested on the seventh day. Therefore the LORD blessed the Sabbath day and made it holy.
FIVE
"Honor your father and your mother, so that you may live long in the land the LORD your God is giving you.
SIX
"You shall not murder.
SEVEN
"You shall not commit adultery.
EIGHT
"You shall not steal.
NINE
"You shall not give false testimony against your neighbor.
TEN
"You shall not covet your neighbor's house. You shall not covet your neighbor's wife, or his manservant or maidservant, his ox or donkey, or anything that belongs to your neighbor."

The first four commandments are presented in a different way by Rudolf Steiner, and in the way that he presents the first three we can see why in the window, these are given special prominence.

Rudolf Steiner's presentation of the commandments

ONE: I am the Eternal Divine which you sense within your own being. I have led you out of Egypt, wherein you were unable to follow Me within yourself. From henceforth you shall not recognize, as divine higher gods, anything that is a representation to you of something in the heavens or something which is active on the Earth, or between the heavens and Earth. You shall not worship anything which is lower than the divine within you. For I am the Eternal within you, and I am the ever self-empowering Divine Being. If you do not recognize Me within you, then shall I, as the Divine, disappear from your children, your grand-children and the great grand-children, and their bodily health shall wither. But if you **do** recognize Me within yourself, then I will live onward as yourself unto the thousandth generation, and the health of your people will prosper.

TWO: You shall not speak error concerning Me within you, for every error regarding the Ego within you, shall injure your body.

THREE: You shall differentiate between the day of labour and the day of rest, so that your existence may be as an image of My existence. For that which lives within you as your self, did create the world in six 'days' and then dwelt within itself on the seventh day. Therefore shall the activity of yourself and of your son, of your daughter, of your servant and of your cattle, be devoted for six days only to external matters, but on the seventh day your gaze shall seek out me within yourself.

FOUR: Continue the work of your father and mother, so that which they possessed as theirs, may become your inheritance, for they gained this through the strength which I formed within them.

FIVE: Do not commit murder.
SIX: Do not commit adultery.
SEVEN: Do not steal.
EIGHT: Do not detract from your neighbour by speaking what is untrue concerning him.
NINE: Do not look covetously upon that which is your neighbour's possession.
TEN: Do not look with covetous eyes upon your neighbour's wife, nor on his servants, nor on the creatures through which he comes to his success.

Here in this central panel with its depiction of the 10 Commandments, the suggestion is given that a person who has died shall discover that the first three Commandments, which are about the sense of self, and one's relation to the Divine, are the very important themes for the soul whose life has ended. Just how a person has lived their life, in regard to the first three of these, in regard to trying to bring the spirit or higher self to birth within their own ego-sense, shall be of great significance for their existence in the after-life. The implication is, that those people who have sought to develop themselves deeply, can expect a profoundly blessed outcome.

NORTH PURPLE WINDOW: PART TWO

*** The Bull forces and an 'emerging bovine'**

Forces from Taurus have been instrumental in bringing about the dense, material world; and the bovines embody this force. This 'Taurus' nature we need, in order to be incarnate, but it is this same force which induces a sensual, earth-bound heaviness in the soul. This is a complex subject, which cannot be examined in detail here. Its complexity is echoed in ancient Egyptian texts which hail the sun god as "as a bull that slays bulls", meaning that the Divine, (the sun god, who was active through the sign of Taurus in ancient Egyptian times, and thus referred to as the sacred bull) helps the acolyte overcome the debased bull forces.[78] The sensual drive of the bull is a force that burdens the human being, degrading the desires; and we noted that the overcoming of this was indicated in the red window.

This negative impact of the Taurean bovine energies upon the human soul is indicated in ancient Egyptian esoteric texts, where the bull is referred to as "the slayer of Osiris" {the sun god}, and, "if a man (on the spiritual path) sees himself (in a dream) slaying a bovine, this is a good sign, for

[78] Inscription on the Piye stele, trans. J Assman 2009.

he is overcoming his {inner} battle-adversary".[79] As a result of this, human beings darken and debase this force from Taurus, which causes a subtle stress for this species; the bovine is freed from this when a person dies. So the springing-forth of a cow or bull in this window is depicting both the release for the bovines from the burden that human beings place upon them, as well as a giving up by the human being of the forces, no longer needed, that gave them a useable physical body. In Nature there is a very good side to the bovine, and this is embodied in the cows. As Rudolf Steiner taught, "when a cow dies, then the spiritual reality which the cow has within it, is capable of being absorbed by the earth, to the benefit of all life on Earth".[80]

*** MOSES**

When we were exploring the south Green Window, we noted the event of Moses encountering Deity speaking from the burning bush. The Hebrew expression in the Book of Exodus (3:14) where Moses is kneeling before the burning bush, *ehyeh asher ehyeh,* (אֶהְ ֶיה אֲשֶׁר אֶהְ ֶיה) has a complex reference to Deity, and by implication it is saying that God and the human higher ego, encompasses the past, the present and the future. These sayings are in effect declaring: *I am, was and shall be,* ***that*** *I am, and shall be*; but with the understanding that this "I am" is referring to what is present in a germinal form in the human being, also. The following brief extract from a lecture about Moses from Rudolf Steiner, from an esoteric point of view, comments on this understanding that the Deity whom Moses is presenting as the source of our higher-self is the 'cosmos Spirit', meaning the highest of the sun gods, or the cosmic Christ,

> The human soul {can} feel that it exists dynamically within the {being and} activity of the Spiritual, just as the people of Egypt once felt {*where Moses lived, and was initiated*}. When a person feels with their inner being {*through deep spiritual effort*} that they are in the midst of cosmic spiritual forces, then the soul shall feel that which manifested to Moses, for the first time ever, through clairvoyant consciousness {in the burning bush}. What is perceived then may be regarded as 'the Cosmos-Spirit', {*that is, the high sun god or the 'cosmic Christ' which can be called the 'Weltengrund' – but here the context is confined to our solar system*}.
>
> And {*then one realizes*} what the various nations, through Moses, were given the impulse to move towards {*that is, the divine spiritual potential within oneself*}. And also through Moses, the capacity was assisted for a person to comprehend and experience this Cosmos-Spirit with their mind, as that Being who forms the underlying basis of the various elements that our world consists of.[81]

Rudolf Steiner also taught that Moses encountered, and endeavoured to bring to awareness in people, the higher ego as an expression of the cosmic Christ or the high sun god. And secondly that it is this great Being, whose external manifestation cosmically is in the spiritual sun, from whom our human spirit derives. Humanity owes to Moses – to the kind of higher thinking that he brought into life in himself – the ability to contemplate and think intellectually about Creation in full consciousness.

There is another association with Moses in this window, as Rudolf Steiner taught that until recently this great person was, in some ways, the Judge of the Dead. He comments that it was said in medieval Christianity – and this correlates to the truth – "When the human being dies, they perceive the reflection of the spiritual world as (in) the compilation of commandments from Moses".[82] Rudolf Steiner also taught that gradually this task is becoming that of Christ Himself.[83]

We now move over to the south side of the hall, to contemplate the south Pink Window.

---

[79] E. Otto, *Stierkulte*, p. 2, 6 (in Untersuchungen zur Geschichte und Altertumskunde Aegypten, Leipzig, 1938); and the *Dreambook* of Papyrus Chester-Beatty 3 (Brit. Museum) from about 1220 BC.
[80] GA 230, p. 55.
[81] GA 60, p. 426.
[82] GA 131, p. 80.
[83] GA 101, p. 248.

The south Pink Window

The threshold is veiled

The threshold is revealed

I am beholding the building

The cosmos builds

The building becomes the human being

THE SOUTH PINK WINDOW

Colour

There are three notes from Rudolf Steiner about the colour scheme of the nine windows. Each of these three stipulate the colour pink ('rosa' in German) and not, as is sometimes said, peach-blossom-lilac, or incarnadine. As mentioned in the first chapter, these windows in the second Goetheanum are unfortunately orange in colour, because of a technical difficulty in the glass works.

A brief comment by Rudolf Steiner about the soul-quality of the colour pink is very helpful here: "I feel the fountain of life".[84] These words seem to indicate that the last two windows, through their colour, are meant to be telling the viewer, of a significant progression underlying all nine windows. Red is about the impetus to work toward the future, green is indicative of our earthly personality, blue brings in a mood of piety, purple is like a doorway into the spirit; and lastly, pink speaks of drawing near to the divine, which is the fountain of life. Rudolf Steiner also describes thoughts which derive from devoted, unselfish love as raying forth from the aura in "glorious pink".

Thematic Overview

There is no over-script from Rudolf Steiner for this window, but its theme is about meditation, at a more advanced level.

Brief overview of the three panels

Left panel: a reclining person, a temple and below are three skulls.

Central panel: a person in meditation, a prominent face above them, the spiritual sun and the moon.

Right panel: an upright person, a face, the spiritual sun and below is the moon.

Exploring the south Pink Window

Left Panel

This side panel has two scripts:

Ich schaue den Bau = ***I am beholding the building***

Die Schwelle verhüllt sich = ***The threshold is veiled*** (or, ***veils itself***)

Here we have a person in a somewhat lazy, reclined position who can see a building; this building is reminiscent of the Goetheanum and thus it represents a temple. This person is, metaphorically, in a kind of sleepy state, indicating that they are not functioning in an initiatory consciousness.

The faces above

These faces appear to represent the past lives of this person.[85] For concerning this artistic feature, Rudolf Steiner taught that,

> Above and beyond the head of a human being – when viewed with '*Imagination*' (Psychic-Image Consciousness) – the countenance of that person from their past life can be seen, and further, above that second head, is the head of the person in an earlier past life. In civilizations which still had an instinctive awareness of this fact you find images in art

---

[84] In GA 291, p. 207.

[85] In the original sketch, there are three faces, and a few scratches or lines. So the artist has made an alteration, as there is part of a fourth face in her sketch.

> where behind the head as drawn, and which refers to this lifetime, another somewhat less clearly defined head is drawn and then a third head, less clear still. There are such images as these in Egypt.[86]

However, since this is a panel in which "*the threshold is veiled*" we can conclude that this person does not have any awareness of these past lives. But since they are placed there, and since the left panel is about the given, less perfect situation, it is implied that awareness of this should at some time dawn on the person – and this is what the right panel shows, as we shall see.

The skulls

Below the person are some skulls, which become more prominent the nearer they are to the viewer. In the original sketch Rudolf Steiner drew two skulls and just the small portion of the lower jawbone of a third skull. But he did see the picture with its three skulls from which the glass was carved, made by the artist, so he approved of altering the sketch into three skulls. To understand these skulls we need to realize that the dark area in which they are placed, is the same as the dark area in the left panel of the red window, under that confused person. That is, the dark vertical area represents the subconscious parts of the soul.[87] So the skulls here are pointing to the as yet un-purified forces of the threefold soul. So they are in effect, pointing to spiritual 'death'. They are placed in the un-illumined field, indicating the subconscious.

So the person is "*beholding the building*" in a sleepy, non-perceptive way; the opposite is portrayed in the right panel. Therefore here the person is simply seeing the physical building, and not the deep mystery embodied in its architecture, so *"The threshold is veiled"*.

The striped background

The field of vision for the 'sleepy one' is light coloured, with dark stripes. To understand this we need firstly to note that the striped background in the right panel is the reverse of this left panel. The reason for this will be clear when explore the right panel.

The central panel of the south Pink Window

Keynote script: ***Die Welt baut*** = ***The cosmos builds***

The spiritual sun

In this central panel, we see a wonderful sight: a person seated in meditation, and behind them the spiritual sun is shining powerfully. It is these rays from the spiritual sun which are making visible a large countenance, with the moon behind it, above the meditating person. This scene is depicting the profound mystery of the higher-self coming into being, arising from the person. This has been made possible by her or his substantial spiritual striving. This has brought them near to the spiritual sun, whose radiance actually brings into visibility so to speak, the higher self. Also the rays from the seated meditant curving up to, and in effect forming, the large face, indicate how **this greater, cosmic self arises from the personality, as it ennobles itself** and as the person enters into a meditative state. The scene here also points out that the higher-self is interwoven into the cosmos. Rudolf Steiner speaks of the spiritual sun shining within a person's aura as they achieve steps on the path to deep spirituality.

The Moon

The moon often symbolizes the night-time, and therefore the cosmos into which we go when we are asleep. Here it may be indicating two things. Firstly, when through meditation (not sleep) the person enters into the cosmos, so to speak, they can become more aware of their higher self, rather than being unconscious. Secondly, it points to the situation, that when the spiritual seeker is in the cosmos, in meditation, he or she is more able to be illumined by the spiritual sun.

---

[86] GA 234, p. 95.

[87] Not literally the soil and rocks deep in the ground.

The stars above sun and moon

Here the stars above the sun take on a more circular form, but those above the moon are in a more linear pattern. This is the same feature as we noted in the Red Window, where these energies were depicted in the etheric and astral aura of the acolyte, so these are influences beyond the physical plane. The lunar energies ray out in a linear way; but the sun's energies well forth in a circular pattern. It is clear that here the view is from a spiritual perspective, not from the physical world. (So the depiction of the sun and moon in the Red and Pink windows is the opposite to that in the north Blue Window, where the view is from the physical world.)

The skull

Beneath the meditating person, there is a decaying skull. It is a well-known physiological fact, that cells of the body die away as the result of physical or mental activities. In particular, here the viewer is being told that this also happens when thoughts are created, or received, especially those of a higher kind.[88]

The right panel of the south Pink Window

This panel has two scripts:

Und Der Bau Wird Mensch = ***And the building becomes the human being***

Die Schwelle offenbart sich = ***The threshold reveals itself***

Both side panels are about a temple, as a symbol of something sacred – the human soul and spirit. With such a subject, this window presents a theme which is found in the Bible (1 Kings:6), and was taken up into Freemasonry. A temple can be described as having certain proportions and unusual decorative features; in earlier times, these features usually symbolized the human soul as it evolves itself up towards the Spirit, or perhaps the relationship of the soul to the cosmos. But the symbolic features of the Goetheanum (and king Solomon's temple) are suggesting that these powers of the soul derive from the cosmos: that is, from the solar system and the zodiac. In this way, the person who is contemplating such a temple begins to realize that cosmic influences are active in their soul and spirit.

When the person becomes spiritually awake, they can experience such questions in their soul as: what is their past, what has brought them into the present, and where are they going, in the future? Such a person is not sleepy, but awakened, and therefore one could describe this as having 'gone across a threshold' into spiritual realms, from the material world. It is this inner alertness which is portrayed in the right panel, by the person being upright and gazing out intently at something. But in addition, the scene here shows us that this inner alertness, or indeed, awakening, has now enabled him or her to start using the seven-stringed lyre. The lyre itself is too indistinct to be seen, but the artist Assia Turgenieff, reported that the person is definitely holding such a lyre. What does this mean?

The Lyre of Apollo

The seven-stringed lyre is a core feature in Greek myths of Apollo the sun god, and his devotee, Orpheus. This lyre symbolizes the soul as derived from the solar system: that is, influences of the seven planets have contributed to the formation of the soul. To be able to play the seven-stringed lyre was used in ancient esoteric religions to means to 'be initiated', because it symbolized the ability to work with, that is to ennoble, the forces from the seven planets which are operative in one's soul (these qualities are revealed by the horoscope). Consequently, it is known that in the Persian esoteric religion of Mithra, a lyre player was used to depict the First Degree initiate. A statue depicting this has survived in Spain, see illustration 18. But in Greece, the lyre, as a symbol of high spiritual consciousness, is also a prominent feature in the myths of Apollo and Orpheus.

---

[88] GA 156, p. 124, lecture 19th Dec. 1914.

The legends about these players tell of how they could tame wild animals by playing on a seven-stringed lyre, and this refers directly to the conquering of the lower qualities in the soul, see illustration 18. Rudolf Steiner explains this lyre as "the inner nature of the human being as a living instrument which reflects back the harmonies and melody {resonating} in the cosmos."[89] He further explains the seven-stringed lyre as also representing, within the physical body,

> ...the nervous system raying out from the backbone; these are a reflection of the cosmic forces which have formed us, condensed into nerve substance. **The soul-spiritual part of that human being who has attained some spiritual enlightenment plays on these strings of the human lyre, within the earthly world.**[90] (emphasis mine, AA)

So, the advanced meditant today can now sense, perceive, and work with, the sevenfold planetary forces. He or she can now see to it that the lower planetary forces from the seven planets, as shown to them by the stern Guardian entity of the north Green Window, are purified. We still have to discover what this higher stage of spirituality now enables the initiate to perceive. In this panel, the person is shown as perceiving a striking face. What does this mean? To understand it, we have to understand another feature in the panel – the area beneath the face. Firstly, we note that this is the exact opposite of the same area in the left panel.

In the right panel, this area is illumined; and also the striped area underneath the face is now dark, with some bright stripes. In this way, the area here in the right panel is the reverse, or the counter-image, of the empty area underneath the temple in the left panel. This means the right panel is indicating that an opposite dynamic applies to what is presented in the left, for there the person is depicted as not inwardly awakened, or 'sleepy' in a certain sense. So here in this panel the person is awakened and thus able to consciously perceive spiritual realities. This awareness and capacity to perceive spiritually allows them see a face, instead of a building. As we shall soon see, this face represents the Higher Self. So the script for this panel starts to take on its real meaning: "*And the building becomes a human being*".

The temple as a symbol of the Spiritual-self

Here we encounter a theme which is also found in Masonic literature. Superficially a temple is simply a temple, a building for religious purposes, which may have various intriguing shapes and decorative features. But perceived more deeply, the architecture of such temples as the Goetheanum and of King Solomon's Temple, as described in the Bible, are symbolic presentations of cosmic influences active in the soul and in the Higher Self, or Spirit-self. For example, the first Goetheanum had two large domes which intersected each other. But placed in the ground as a foundation stone, was an iron pyrites crystal which was a double dodecahedron (or double twelve-sided shape). The implication is that the two domes are rounded-out dodecahedra; one smaller than the other.

Symbolically, this feature represents the creation and nurturing of the human being from the cosmos, which means really from the twelve zodiac influences; and we human beings do have in subtle ways, twelve-sides to our nature. Inside the Goetheanum are seven huge pillars. These represent the sevenfold nature of humanity. This includes the seven basic elements that make up the human being, which we mentioned in the section of the north Blue Window; and the seven-year phases of life that we go through. Evidence for having higher consciousness is also seen in the area below the person standing with their lyre.

The three faces and moon

We noted how in the left panel there are three skulls underneath the non-initiated person, and they are placed in a dark area. We also noted that this dark area is the subconscious part of the soul, not the ground beneath our feet. On the left, in daylight (the bright area with thin dark stripes) the person can see the physical temple; but the dark area with the skulls indicates they

---

[89] GA 283, p. 83.

[90] GA 106, p. 94 and GA 291, p.173.

18 The initiate lyre-player

Above left: a rare statue of the 1st degree initiate in the Mithraic Mysteries. Found in Spain, the inscription reads in part: "*to the invincible deity Mithra*"; from ca. AD 155.

Above right: A simple painting of Orpheus from the Christians in the catacombs; 4th century AD.

Above: Orpheus tames the savage beasts; a Roman mosaic from ca. AD 194.

have their lower qualities veiled in the subconscious part of the soul. They also have indicators of their past lives hovering above them. But here in the right panel, the subconscious is now illumined; so the unredeemed lower qualities, which deaden consciousness, symbolized as the skulls, have now been removed. The lower qualities had been perceived and as a result, they have been transformed. In addition, the three faces which were hovering above the temple in the left panel, are now integrated into the soul. This indicates that this person has developed perception of their past lives. So as part of a higher consciousness, the various past lives have now been accessed and integrated. Below these three faces is the moon.

The moon here appears to be alluding to a Biblical image found in the Book of Revelation, where a woman, who represents the Spiritual-self, has the stars around her head, but the moon at her feet. As Rudolf Steiner explains in lectures about the Book of Revelation, this means that the soul has trampled down the lower-self; it is conquered. So in this right panel, this person has achieved a higher consciousness; and what they are seeing now is their Higher Self. We remember here that the script for the right panel is: *The threshold reveals itself.* The consciousness of this person is crossing over threshold, into spiritual worlds. The person is playing their lyre, or consciously integrating and experiencing their sevenfold soul, and thus its cosmic origins – and this will bring a person to perception of their Higher Self. What are some other indicators that the prominent face seen here, is the Higher-self?

Serapis: ancient Egyptian initiation

The face, with a plant-like form arising from its head, is a metamorphosis of an ancient image of the Spiritual-self used in the initiatory Mysteries of Serapis, in ancient Egypt. This high initiation religion was transplanted into Greece by Ptolemy I, and most of the images of Serapis that have survived, are from the Hellenistic Age, see illustration 19. The various carvings from the cult of Serapis show a noble head, on top of which are several plants. In order to have these plants securely placed above the head, they are carved on to a short cylinder. The meaning of this striking image is unknown to academic scholars, as it was kept secret in the ancient Mysteries. But Rudolf Steiner's high praise of the Serapis Mysteries indicates that deep initiatory truths were its focus, "...the deep teachings which were brought to expression in...the gazing up to Serapis."[91] He confirms that it came into being in ancient Egypt, and was only later brought into the Grecian culture. Before exploring the meaning of this plant-like form arising from the head, let's just confirm that Rudolf Steiner did make use of ancient Egyptian art, in his own artwork.

That Rudolf Steiner drew on, and integrated ancient Egyptian esoteric ideas and art in his teachings, is reflected in the Egyptian scarab-beetle pendant which he designed, see illustration 20. The scarab beetle rolls decaying matter along, and places its eggs in it, from which new beetles emerge. It became a core image in esoteric Egyptian religion, as it represented the arising of new life out of decaying matter; this had similarities to the sun which rolls across the sky and is re-born in the morning. But it can also represent the Spiritual-self as it is created out of the temporary, lower-self, which fades away.

Of this jewellery item, Rudolf Steiner said, "the scarab beetle is bearing the sun hither in front of itself" [92] – exactly the same dynamic that the beetle represented in ancient Egypt. But we notice that the ruby in the pendant is a pentagram, and in anthroposophy this represents, as we have noted earlier, the Spiritual-self. So both the ancient Egyptian meaning and the anthroposophical view, are inherent in the version designed by Rudolf Steiner.

Such use of ancient Egyptian esoteric wisdom is quite natural to anthroposophy. This is because, as Rudolf Steiner taught, the esoteric wisdom arising in anthroposophy, and also elsewhere in the modern era, is linked to ancient Egypt. He taught that it is itself the result of ancient Egyptian initiation wisdom re-emerging in people today. This is possible because there are some people who had achieved high spiritual insights in Egyptian secret wisdom, who are re-born into today's world; he mentions Paracelsus and Johannes Kepler in this regard.[93]

---

[91] GA 237, p.126.
[92] In German, "Der Scarabäus trage die Sonne (den Rubin) vor sich her".
[93] GA 106, p.170, and GA 113, p. 155.

19 Enlivened consciousness symbolized as life-forces in (arising from) the head

Above: Two images of Serapis

Above left: a painting on wood from Roman times; about AD 100, from Egypt, in the J.P. Getty Museum.

Above right: a carved image from Carthage, Tunisia; about AD 230; in the Louvre, Paris.

Below : the same theme from the Druids. A scene from the Gundestrup Cauldron; the initiate has achieved an enlivened consciousness.

20 Egyptian scarab pendant designed by Rudolf Steiner

Here the ancient Egyptian spiritual symbol of the scarab beetle is nurturing a 5-sided ruby, which here is used as a symbol of the Spirit-self, the eternal spirit in the human being, which sends the personality back to re-birth.

So it appears very likely that the image of plants growing on the head is pointing to the same high stage of spirituality as does the face in the pink window, where plant-like energies are streaming up from the head. Such an image points to the capacity to experience high spiritual insights, and these in turn vitalize the etheric energies: that is, the etheric body becomes transformed through the effect of high spirituality in the soul.

This transformation of the etheric forces in a highly spiritual person was well-known in antiquity; it was not limited to Egypt and Greece. The ancient Druids, whose greatest sacred site was the Externsteine in northern Germany, were aware of this, too. European people involved in Mystery centres and esoteric wisdom, used the reindeer with it antlers, as a sacred symbol, because its etheric body is unusual. For reindeer's life-forces are naturally powerful in the head area, where normally there is little life-force in any living creature. This is why human beings and most animals have little capacity to heal and rejuvenate the head area. At the Externsteine site, the Druids carved a large deer, in reference to this phenomenon.[94]

But the Druids also had another major site: this was in the Rhodope mountains of Bulgaria. And it is in this site that another esoteric sacred Druidic artwork was crafted. This is a cauldron made of pure silver, which was found in 1891, hidden in the ground, in Denmark. Known as the Gundestrup Cauldron, it is dated to about 100 BC, and it shows explicitly the enlivening of consciousness in the initiate. One of the twelve panels of carvings on this silver cauldron depicts an initiate who has gained the stage of consciousness that the pink window depicts, which is linked to the enlivened etheric body, which the reindeer naturally have. The initiate is depicted as having reindeer horns growing from his head, see illustration 19.

Now the question arises, why do the two side panels of this window refer to progressing up to seeing the Higher Self? What relevance does this achievement have to the central panel ? The progress from the left to the right panel reveals what has made the central panel possible. If a person can discover a symbolic, artistic presentation of their Higher-self in a temple's architecture, then they are on the path to livingly experience the Spiritual-self in their meditation. Then they will start to experience, firstly, how human beings have a Higher Self. Secondly, they will discover that this Spiritual-self has a cosmic structure ! In the words of Rudolf Steiner, "***The temple: that is the human being who receives into his soul, the Spirit.***"[95] The Spiritual-self is formed from the cosmos, from the noble influences of the planets, and especially from the radiance of the spiritual sun, hence: '***the cosmos builds***'.

We can now walk across to the north Pink Window.

---

[94] To know more about the Externsteine, see the book, *The Externsteine* by Damien Pryor.

[95] GA 286, p.24.

The north Pink Window

In this way, he becomes holy

The cosmos is enfilled with holiness

The holiness is efficacious

THE NORTH PINK WINDOW

Thematic Overview
There is no over-script from Rudolf Steiner for this window, but its theme includes the significance of the Christ-reality, and of advanced meditation.

Brief overview of the three panels
Left panel: Golgotha hill with the three crosses, and two spirit beings up in the air.

Central panel: an Angel, a person gazing at something, and a prominent face, the spiritual sun.

Right panel: Golgotha hill with the three crosses, and two beings inside the Earth.

This is the last of the nine windows, and it has been understood as depicting what Rudolf Steiner called the "Reappearing of Christ in the etheric".[96] But we shall see that it does not depict this important dynamic, but something else. To discover the message of this window, it will be helpful if we start to explore the two side panels, and after considering the central panel, return to them again.

Exploring the north Pink Window

Left Panel

Keynote script: ***So wird er fromm*** = ***In this way, he becomes holy **** (* or, pious)

Here, and in the right panel, we are seeing an event undertaken by Christ during the time that the body of Jesus was on the cross. This event was known in the first centuries of Christianity as the "Harrowing of Hades"; this is an old English term which means to undertake actions against evil powers in their realm. This very old religious or theological idea is actually in the Bible; it is in the Gospels and in some Epistles. This now-neglected aspect of the mission of Christ, was understood to be an action undertaken against evil; specifically against 'the Devil' or 'Satan'. If you are new to Rudolf Steiner's teachings, you will be surprised to learn that he taught that these two terms actually refer to two different kinds of fallen spiritual Powers. These are the ones we have already discussed: Lucifer and Ahriman. We noted then that Lucifer has to do with excessive personal pride and sensuality and naïve thinking; he is the being meant by the term, 'the Devil'. And Ahriman we noted, has to do with a cold self-centred way of thinking and of will: and thus with crime. He is the being who is meant by the term, 'Satan'.

It is central to esoteric Christianity, as taught by Rudolf Steiner, that the events on Golgotha hill were such that the influence of both Lucifer and Ahriman were weakened, and also the Earth's aura was permeated by a divine radiance. There are passages in the New Testament which either affirm this or directly support this. One such passage which refers to this is in the Epistle of Peter; although Christians reading this in translation may not be aware of it. But the reader of the Greek text is told that whilst the body was on the cross, Christ went in his soul-spirit body and gave teachings and spiritual aid to those souls whose body had died recently. Correctly translated, Peter 4:5,6 is saying as follows:

ὅι ἀποδώσουσιν λόγον τῷ ἑτοίμως ἔξοντι κρῖναι
...they {the Dead} shall give an account to the One having readiness to judge
ζῶντας καί νεκρούς
living persons and dead persons*. (*in literary English, *'the souls of the dead')*
εἰς τοῦτο γάρ καί νεκροῖς εὐηγγελίσθη,

[96] This theory appears to derive from S. Prokofieff, in "*The Twelve Holy Nights and the Spiritual Hierarchies.*"

For this is the reason the gospel was also preached to dead persons [97]
ἵνα κριθῶσι μέν
that they may be judged indeed
κατά ἀνθρώπους σαρκί
as to the flesh, according to human nature,
ζῶσι δέ κατά θεόν πνεύματι
but {that} they may exist as to the spirit, according to God."

This passage does not mention taking action against fallen spirits, but it opens the possibility for this to be happening also, and then a little later on St. Peter says that indeed Christ also "went to the spirits in prison" (τοῖς ἐν θυλακῇ πνεύμασιν); the term 'spirits' infers fallen spirit entities.

In the left panel, we see Christ rising up into the air, to weaken the influence that Lucifer exerts on humanity. The moon above refers to Lucifer's past, as this entity spiritually fell in what is known as the Moon Aeon. This is the third of the four aeons of evolution that we have journeyed through. Also, in terms of romantic illusions that exist in the earthly ego-sense, it is the night-time, symbolized by the moon, when Lucifer's power is enhanced. That the moon is waning here points to the waning power of Lucifer as a result of the deeds of Christ. The three bright streams flowing upwards in this panel, point to the redeeming influence of the cosmic Christ permeating the ether and astral aura of the Earth.

The right panel shows the other action of Christ in the "Harrowing" of Hell": that is, his activity designed to weaken and imprison the Ahrimanic beings. This takes place deep inside the Earth. We shall look at the implications of this, after we explore the central panel, and learn about an ancient esoteric Christian text that actually specifies that these two groups of beings were dealt with by Christ, during the Golgotha event.

The central panel of the north Pink Window

Keynote script: ***Die Welt weht Frommsein = The cosmos is enfilled with holiness*** (or piety)

More literally, *A sense of holiness is gently flowing-forth from Creation, or, The world around about me has a living ambience of holiness (or, piety)*

The central panel has the final message for the person walking through the Great Hall. From the left and right panels, one sees that the path to spiritual development is deeply linked to the deeds of Jesus Christ. The reader will have already noticed that this theme is very important in anthroposophical wisdom, even though anthroposophy is not a religion. The name 'Jesus Christ' is understood in anthroposophical wisdom as referring to the human being whose self or 'ego-sense' was raised to the highest kind possible, from the presence of the cosmic sun-god, Christ, in Jesus. We noted earlier that this view, which derives from Rudolf Steiner's research, is regarded in the religion of Christianity as a heresy. This presence within Jesus of the sublime sun god from whom, in the first instance, the human spirit derives, was brought about through the Baptism in the Jordan, and especially through the Resurrection. Jesus then became the archetype of what human beings are intended to become in the far future, and this archetype is needed to make possible humanity's path up to this high level of being.[98]

Now the question arises here, just what does the central panel depict?

The Large Countenance

Certainly the large countenance appearing here is close to some plants, and, as we saw in the south Purple Window, such a feature is locating the activity in the etheric world. So now, we need

[97] The reason that translations of this passage say "*For this is the reason the gospel was preached even to those who are* ***now*** *dead..*" is that church translators specifically add the word for "now", to avoid the esoteric meaning.
[98] See my Rudolf Steiner Handbook for more about this theme.

to contemplate the 'artistic gesture' of the artwork here, and especially of the large face. But, also as part of this task, we need to be clear about just exactly what is carved in the lower sector of this pane of glass. On the far left, in the darker area, and not easy to see, there is a malignant being, who represents what is left of the lower-self of the acolyte. This being was carved into the window by Assia Turgenieff, following the sketch from Rudolf Steiner. Then there is the Angel of this person. The Angel is doing two things. Firstly it is acting as a protection for the acolyte from the (now weaker) lower-self or Double; secondly it is doing the equivalent of what we can do physically when we take a friend by the shoulders and turn them to face something. The Angel is specifically helping the acolyte to become aware of something.

And the 'gesture' of the acolyte's arms, of reaching out, tells us that his or her soul is reaching out to cognize (or perceive) this 'something'. Here in this panel, artistically, the gesture of this countenance is of a delicate, tenuous quality, rather like a blossom unfolding. This face has closed eyes, which is not the gesture of a being with mighty inner power and spiritual capacity, such as divine beings have. So what then is this face representing?

It represents the beginnings of a capacity to perceive in the etheric; and this leads to being able to function in the ether, as it were. This is a capacity in the meditating person to perceive spiritually through their etheric energies, and not through the body's sensory organs. One could also say, the capacity to function in the etheric realm. Once this happens, "*We become aware of a 'second person' in us*", as Rudolf Steiner describes it. He said about this,

> We learn to cognize how the etheric forces flow in and out, and how everything which there, outside, is a play of universal forces, is the same thing which, in us, is a shadow-image, producing {earthly} thinking.[99]

So as etheric perception arises the contact to the Spirit is made and these shadow-images, or mental images, give way to direct, living thought-forms as he explained in 1917,

> the essential point is, that the soul-spiritual element can only come into a connection with the physical, through the etheric body...and it is in this way that it is possible for a real raising of oneself (of one's consciousness) to that which is immortal in the human being....the Eternal-Spiritual part of the human being in this way, via the etheric, comes into connection with the part of the human being that dies and becomes re-born.[100]

As he further commented in 1923, about this advanced consciousness condition,

> one feels that one is within a subtler, second person.... 'I experience myself in an etheric body, in a body of finer, more tenuous {energy-}substance'...a second person {is there} and through this etheric body....the meditant can perceive a new world, one which is not accessible to the physical body.[101]

So here we see the acolyte beginning to sense his consciousness expanding into the etheric realm, as if he is confronting a second person that belongs to himself: this is the countenance depicted here in the etheric. This is the stage from which clairvoyance starts, and this blessed state draws the person towards the spiritual sun. And here the rays of the sun appear to be drawing the acolyte towards itself, rather than simply radiating outwards. It is this condition which could be described as, "*The world around about me has a living ambience of the sacred*".[102]

The Spiritual Sun

This feeling of the world around one being permeated by a feeling of holiness, arises as the meditant develops higher consciousness, giving him or her an awareness in their etheric energies as to what is drawing near to them from spiritual realms. And here the scene is telling us,

---

[99] From GA 84, p. 82 lecture 15th April 1923.
[100] GA 66, ps. 170-71, lecture 17th Mar. 1917.
[101] From GA 84, ps.274-5, lecture 26th May 1924.
[102] This scene is not about Jesus re-appearing in the ethers, in a process usually called *The Second Coming of Jesus.*

through the very prominent presence of the spiritual sun, that this heightened awareness is being sustained by, and is also due to, spiritual Powers from the sun-sphere. Already in the red window's right panel the spiritual sun was portrayed as the goal, and here in the last window it is again prominent.

But the importance of the spiritual energies from the heart of the solar system, the sun-sphere, is further emphasized by the two side panels. For this wonderful achievement of "*The World around about me has a living ambience of the sacred*", has been made possible for the meditant, by the action indicated in the left panel: "*In this way, he becomes holy".* It is through the help from the great sun-spirit provided during the Golgotha events, whereby Lucifer's influence was weakened, that the meditant can attain to holiness (that is, spirituality). The message of the right panel goes further. It declares that the spirituality attained by the meditant is stronger; it has a power within it to affect the world around one, for the better. This scene is then very organically linked to the process of spiritual development or self-initiation, which the other windows are about.

The five stars

Above the spiritual sun, there are five stars, two of which are permeated by the rays from the spiritual sun. These appear to represent, like the five stars in the north Green Window, the soul of the person. Together with the sun and moon, these seven form the classical 'seven planets' of the horoscope. Here they appear to be saying that now the soul of the meditant is permeated by noble spiritual influences from the spiritual sun.

The Moon is waxing

When we are awake, the physical sun shines outwardly upon us. To understand this feature, we just need to understand what the moon indicated in the south Pink Window. Rudolf Steiner taught that when we are asleep, the spiritual sun shines within our soul. The moon represents the night-time, when we are out of our body, dreaming. But as the self-initiation process progresses, then it is as if a *second person* develops within us, and the result of this inner presence, is that our dreams become ever more meaningful.

The right panel of the north Pink Window

Keynote script: ***Die Frommheit wirkt*** = ***Holiness is efficacious*** (*or, piety is efficacious*)

Here we see the second phase of *The Harrowing of Hades.* As we noted earlier, Christ also descended into the Earth to enchain Ahriman, as it were. The perception that the Earth's interior is a malignant area, on the astral level, was widespread in earlier times; for example in the Old Testament, King David refers to criminals as persons who shall, after death, be taken down into these subterranean depths: "Those who seek to take my life shall be destroyed; they shall go down into the depths of the earth." (Psalm 63:9) And the Book of Job locates Satan (or Ahriman) in the Earth's sinister, gloomy interior, "The Lord said to Satan, 'Whence comest thou?' Then Satan answered the Lord, 'From going to and fro inside the Earth and from walking up and own inside it'." Awareness of this situation can be found in literature from Homer through to Shakespeare.

Whereas the moon was prominent in the left panel, here it is the sun which is prominent. One reason for this is, that the malignant entity Ahriman fell in an aeon, (or large evolutionary phase), earlier than the one in which Lucifer morally fell. This aeon is called the 'Sun aeon'. With the influence from the spiritual sun, directed by the sun god Christ against Ahriman, weakening his power, the persistent spiritual seeker is helped to conserve their life-forces, and thereby subtly bestow an inner strength onto their spirituality. This bestows on such a person a capacity to bring about a tangible spiritual awareness in their fellow human beings; and an intensified capacity for powerful inspiration in their work. So in essence this window proclaims a core anthroposophical teaching, about the sun god Christ: namely **that this divine being is now the primary guiding being within the aura of the Earth**, and this dynamic offers profound opportunities to the spiritual seeker.

A Coptic poetic text, from about AD 350, has survived in Egypt, from the Manichaeans about the 'Harrowing of Hades'; it is very likely the only text in world literature (apart from Rudolf Steiner's) which proclaims the two-fold redeeming action undertaken by the cosmic Christ. See the Appendix for the full text of this esoteric poetic hymn. An extract from this hymn follows:

> ....Then the sun withdrew it's light.
> It wore a mantle of grief.
> But He arose from those murderers,
> He was caught up from their presence.
> And He bound Them of the sky by the fear of His light:
> He bound Them of the air,
> By the power of His Angels.
> And He bound Them in the earth by the marvel of His cross.
> The doors and bars of the souls in Hades He broke apart;
> He shone forth with His light upon the darkness that is without light
> A new radiance was seen beneath the earth....[103]

In conclusion: the sequence of the windows

There is the question, what is the correct sequence to see these windows, as one goes in one's imagination, through the Great Hall of either the first or the second Goetheanum ? My conclusion is that the sequence used in this book is the correct one. The reason for this is that, the south Purple Window, which is speaking about coming into incarnation, must come before the north Purple Window, which is about the end of life. If this conclusion is correct, then the only natural way to move from window to window is through the sequence used here, see illustration 22.

In this sequence, we experience firstly the Red Window which gives us a preview as to the state of the soul when the quest for higher spirituality has been undertaken for some time. Then the south Green Window points to the awakening in one's heart to the true nature of desire. Then moving over to the north Green Window, awareness of the sevenfold Double is pointed out, as part of the awakening as to the shadows in one's thinking and underlying will. Then walking over to the right, to the south Blue Window, the lesson is about one's will, how it can be destructive, and how this contrasts to the selfless will of our creators. It is a lesson that the past and the present can teach us, as we contemplate the creating of humanity over the aeons.

Then, going over to our left, to the north Blue Window, the lesson is about the age-old impulse in humanity to arise above the Earth's animal, astral qualities; it is in effect a challenge to develop perception as to the link between the human soul and the earthly world more consciously – to contemplate the mystery of the Sphinx. We then cross over to the south side of the hall, to the south Purple Window. Here the scenes speak about incarnating into the world, raising the question: what karma has brought us here? Then going to our left, to the north side, we contemplate the north Purple Window. This firstly, reveals the core dynamics about death; how shall we fare in regard to the requirements placed on a soul spiritually, when life is over. Secondly it poses the question, what does the cycle of birth and death really mean?

Then we go to our right, to the south Pink Window, which portrays the decisive changes in one's consciousness when the practice of meditation brings about a cosmic sense of self, and some awareness of the interlinking between the cosmos and our spirit. Finally, as we move to the north side, we encounter the north Pink Window, which firstly speaks of the sense of a second person delicately developing within oneself, bringing about the ability to perceive spiritual truths directly through one's etheric body, no longer dependent upon the physical body.

And secondly, this last window proclaims how this path to cognizing the spiritual, to perceiving in the divine realms, and to living within a world imbued with holiness – a holiness that also permeates the human being – has been made possible through the events on Golgotha hill, carried out by the Christ, as a gift to humanity.

---

[103] From *A Manichaean Hymn Book*, edit. C. Allberry, Kohlhammer Vlg; Stuttgart, 1938, p. 196.

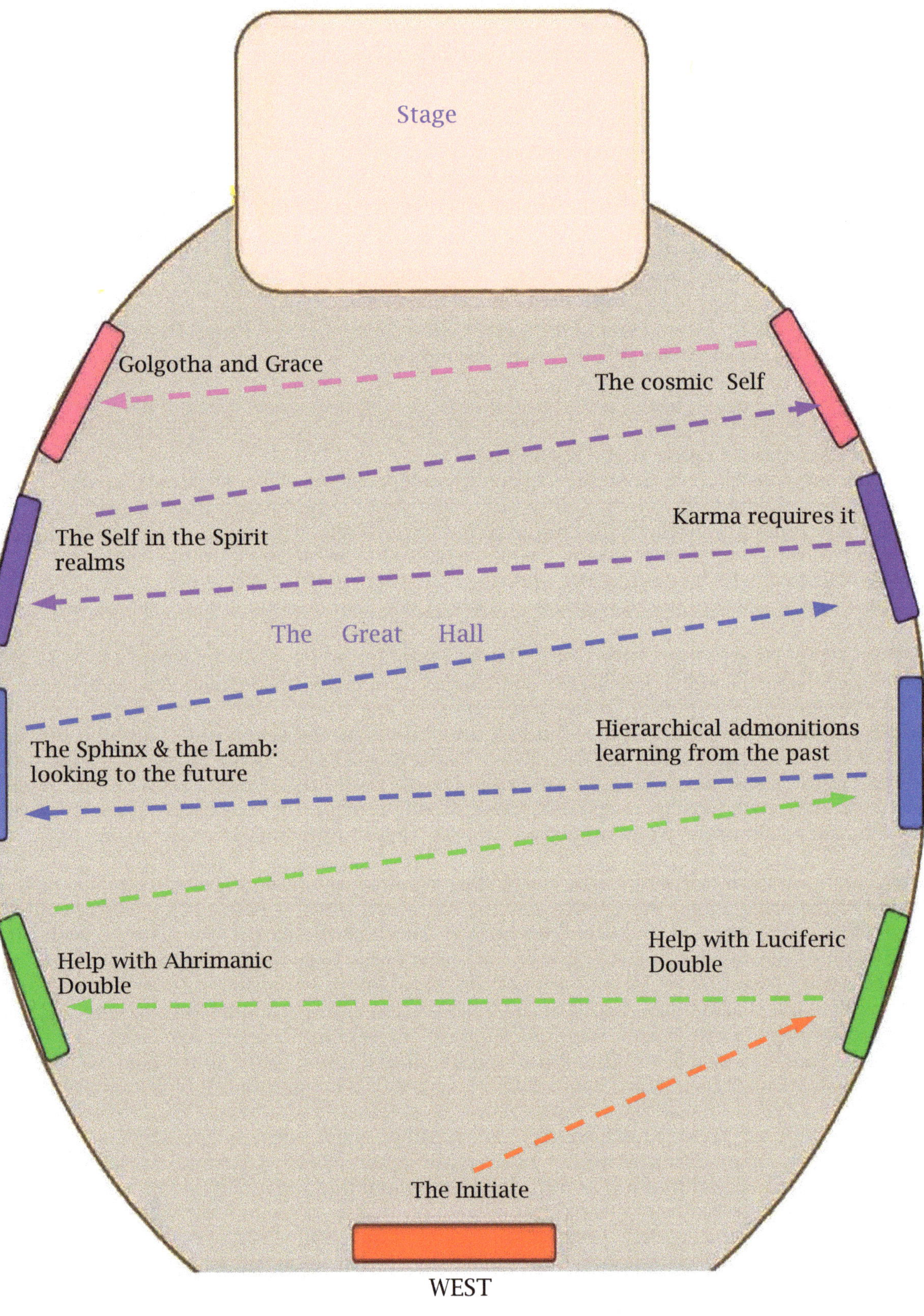

22 **The Sequence through the Goetheanum windows**

Appendix One:

A hymn from an ancient Syriac Manichaean text, preserved in Coptic

The Son of the living God,
The physician of souls,
Let us sing to Him,
The Saviour of spirits,
The Father who is in the Son,
The Son who is in the Father.
God became Man and lived in the world,
The call of His cry went out over the world.
Envy filled the Pharisees.
They gave pieces of silver for Him.
They delivered Him to the Judge although sin was not found in Him.
They hanged Him to the cross at the sixth hour of the day.
They set out to kill Him, so they made Him a monarch.
They crowned Him with thorns because he humbled their kings.
They put a cloak upon Him for He
Stripped the principalities and powers from their authority.
They put a robe of purple upon Him because He confronted their lusts.
They put a reed in His hand because he wrote in the earth of their sins,
They pierced Him with a spear for He destroyed their idols

Then the sun withdrew it's light;
It wore a mantle of grief.
But He arose from those murderers
He was caught up from their presence,
And He bound them of the sky by the fear of His light:
He bound them of the air, of the sky realms
By the power of His Angels.
And He bound them in the earth by the marvel of His cross;
The doors and bars of the souls in Hades He broke apart.
He shone forth with His light upon the darkness that is without light
A new radiance was seen beneath the earth.

His trumpet summoned the multitude of His hosts.
He saved those bound by the Angel of Death.
Death sought in Him, he found nothing belonging to it.
He arose victorious and departed from the powers of Death,
He awakened first the righteous,
He took them with Him into His Father.
He ascended to the right hand of the Father God.
My Saviour, teach me the way to life,
That I may come to Thee rejoicing
For I will to dwell in Thy realms, in the bridal chambers of heavenly light.
Oh hearken to my cry ! Oh hear my prayer !
Glory to Thee my God, my Saviour,
Victory and glory to the soul of the blessed Maria.

(Translated by the editor, C. Allberry)

Appendix Two:

Note: The extraordinary German Emperor Barbarossa, the first emperor of old Germany, lived in the 12th century. A legend was created about him, similar to that of King Arthur – the 'once and future' king. He was, so runs the legend, not dead, but existing in a mysterious way, deep under a Mountain. This mountain is the Untersberg Mt. near Salzburg in Austria, or some say, in the Kyffhaüser Mountains in Thuringia.

****

The Legend of Barbarossa

On the Kyffhaüser Mountains, overlooking the Golden Plain, in the forest of ancient beech and oak trees, stands the ruins of an ancient castle, where Germany's first emperor held court. Here, long centuries ago, Barbarossa ruled over Germany's cities, amidst the fertile farmland hewn out of great forests. Barbarossa's rule did not end with his death, but with his descent deep into the hidden recesses of the Kyffhaüser Mountains. There he waits enchanted, throughout the centuries, until his ravens tell him that the time has come, when he is to again appear before the world and defend the truth and fight for the right. Seated on an ivory throne by a marble table, he rests his head on his arm and his long red beard has grown over the table's edge.

A crown, glittering with diamonds, rests upon his aged head, and from his shoulders the imperial mantel hangs in splendour. His eyes are closed, but at times he seems to awaken from his enchanted rest, and new life appears to animate his stiffened limbs. During these moments he is listening intensely, faintly hearing, deep in his hidden cavern, the cries of the ravens that fly high above the mountain. One day, a holy day in the year, a miner came wandering across the Kyffhaüser, and paused to rest under some ancient beech trees. Immersed in devout reflections, gazing at the ruins of the castle, he suddenly saw, startled, a monk dressed in long robes and cowl, standing near by. The monk addressed him, saying "Come, I have long expected thee; for thou shalt behold the enchanted emperor; no evil shall befall thee."

The monk then led the astonished miner to a secluded green spot, and with his staff he drew a circle around himself and the miner. Then taking an aged book, bound in velvet from his pocket, he began to murmur and chant, no word of which the awed miner understood. Suddenly a mighty clap of thunder pealed out and part of the mountain began to open up, the circle on which they were standing began to sink down ever deeper into the cavity. Terrified the miner clung to the monk as they descended still deeper into the mountain. At length they came to a stop. The monk walked forward along a dark tunnel, the miner following closely behind him, until they reached two huge brass gates. At a touch of the monk's rod these sprang open, giving them entry to an aisle lit by a brilliant lamp; until again after some time they had reached another door. The monk then cried out "Hephaistos", and the door slowly opened. They entered a large magnificent chapel, hewn from marble, with an altar of beaten gold, whereupon an eternal lamp bathed all in a wondrous soft light.

The miner cannot gaze enough at this extraordinary scene; the monk kneels down and prays; and then rising, he commands his companion to remain standing in the middle of the chapel, whilst he moves over to the door opposite the one through which they had entered. Again, at his mighty invocation, this door too opens wide, and the monk enters the imperial throne-room of the emperor. On his glittering throne, clad in royal mantle, Barbarossa is seated – most wise and ageless monarch.

The monk approaches reverently and bows. "What say the ravens. Shall I soon arise ?" Intones the king. "Sire, around the castle-hill I see the ravens flutter and soaring in circles still", responds the monk. "So, if the ancient ravens still circle far and near, then here must I remain, enchanted, yet another hundred years", spoke Barbarossa. The monk then lifts with great solemnity some object from the marble table and again bows low before the monarch. He withdraws slowly to the door, and grasps the hand of the miner who has gazed as if in a dream at the splendour of the enchanted sanctuary. The monk then leads him back to the green circle of earth, which at once begins to rise and soon they reach the secluded spot on the mountain side. The miner gazes

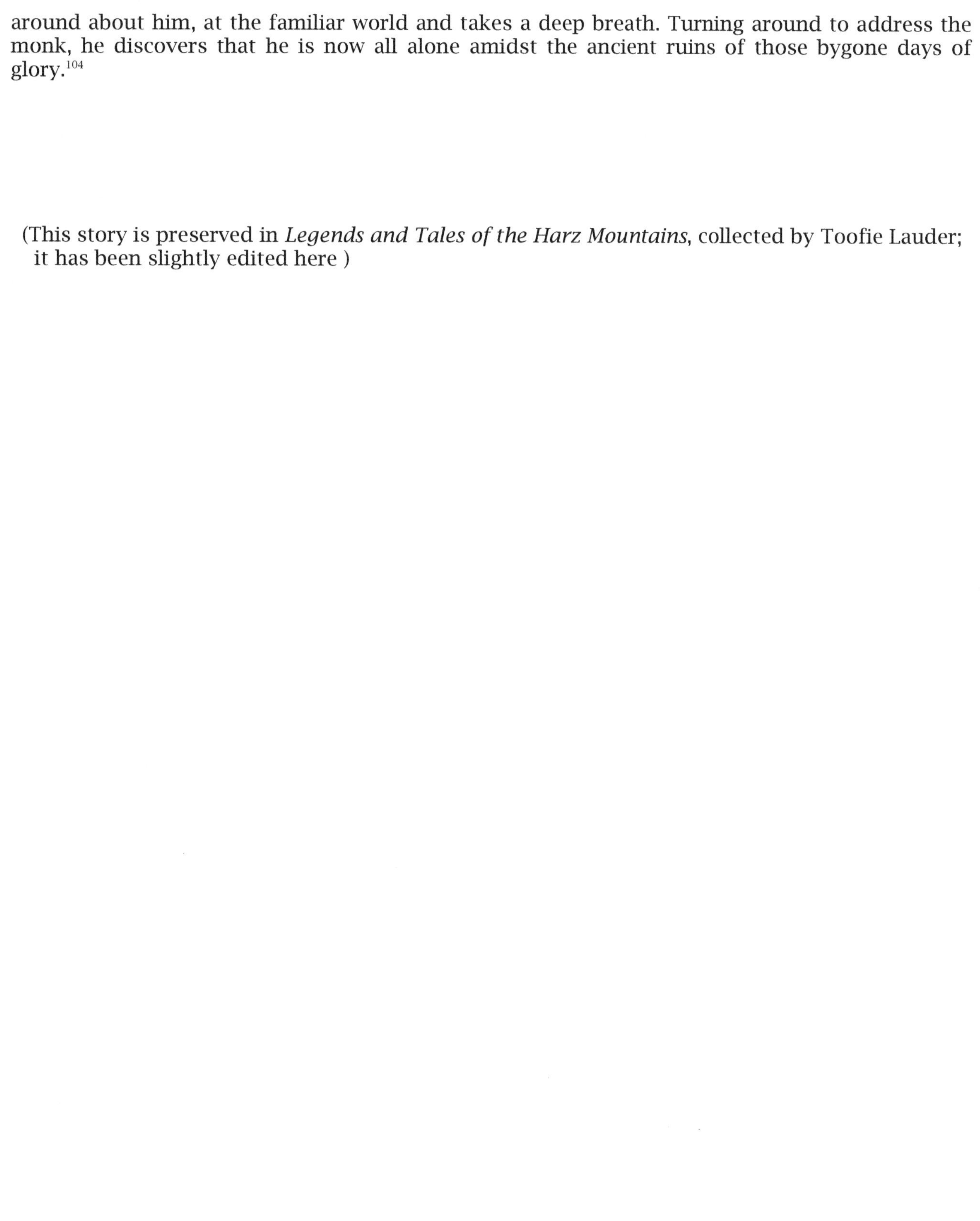

around about him, at the familiar world and takes a deep breath. Turning around to address the monk, he discovers that he is now all alone amidst the ancient ruins of those bygone days of glory.[104]

(This story is preserved in *Legends and Tales of the Harz Mountains*, collected by Toofie Lauder; it has been slightly edited here)

[104] Toofie Lauder, *Legends and Tales of the Harz Mountains*, Hodder & Stoughton, London, 1881.

Appendix Three:

The three colour schemes for the windows, from notebooks of Rudolf Steiner

ONE: 3rd March 1917

ROT	=	RED	
GRÜN	=	GREEN	
BLAU	=	BLUE	
VIOLETTE	=	PURPLE	{*Violet* is, in German, 'blau-violette'.)
ROSA	=	PINK	

****

TWO: undated (p. 47 in H. Raske, *The Language of Colour*)

ROT	=	RED
GRÜN	=	GREEN
BLAU	=	BLUE
LILA	=	LILAC
ROSA	=	PINK

* *

THREE: 1919 - 1920 (In GA 268, p. 253)

ROT	=	RED
GRÜN	=	GREEN
BLAU	=	BLUE
LILA	=	LILAC
ROSA	=	PINK

It is noteworthy that in two of these three schemes, it was specified that the purple windows were to be lilac in colour.

Appendix Four:

Zarathustra and the south Green Window

A comment was allegedly made by Rudolf Steiner to help an enquirer who was having his first experience of the windows. A Dutch member of the Anthroposophical Society reported that when Rudolf Steiner was showing another member around the interior of the Goetheanum as it was being built, this visitor, looking at this south Green Window, asked Steiner, "Who is that venerable man in the left panel?" His question was about the person below, walking with his arms stretched out as if in a religious or esoteric ceremony. It is reported that Rudolf Steiner answered to the effect that, *It is Zarathustra and above him, is the god Ahura Mazdao with the 'Amshaspands'.*[105] (The latter are twelve deities prominent in the Zoroastrian religion, representing the zodiac.)

This report, as with quite a number of indirect reporting of Rudolf Steiner's words in conversation, may not be fully accurate. Such reports can be subject to errors.[106] As we have seen, the purpose of all these windows is to explain core dynamics about spiritual development to people of today's world. And as in the other windows, the person in the left panel represents any spiritually seeking person encountering the imperfections of their soul, and then in the right panel, we are shown how there has been a change, as the person achieves their goal. Then the middle panel shows this acolyte again, but now depicting important elements of either their struggle, or their main achievement. The windows are lessons for people today, and not comments on sages of long ago. My understanding is that Steiner actually answered, in a kindly way, to someone as yet unaware of this inherent triune pattern in each window, that the person below is the great initiate, Zarathustra.

In other words, the visitor was quite new to these extraordinary windows, and hence unaware of their over-all structure. He was unaware that in each of the nine windows the same person is shown in the left, middle and right panels, and the three panels show the spiritual progress or struggles of this same acolyte on the path to spiritual development. So, in view of the non-understanding here, the enquirer was given a kindly answer to his question, about the left panel, by considering it as quite separate from the other two panels (which it isn't in reality). But in this way, for a special purpose, it could be interpreted as Zarathustra in a temple, with the sun god Ahura Mazdao above him, surrounded by twelve zodiac forces. It is possible for Rudolf Steiner to imply that the venerable man and the face above him, which really represent an acolyte and his higher-self, are also Zarathustra and the sun god Ahura Mazdao. This is because, it is true that an initiate (and his deity) are the expression of the higher-self of a spiritual seeker. As Rudolf Steiner taught,

> .... the every-day self must learn that its future state exists now in that which the Initiates, the wise leaders of humanity, have already experienced and which is a signifier of our own future. We must understand that.....we are to see our future self in these initiates. The true higher-self speaks from all beings. Hence from the words of the initiate, my {higher} self also speaks to me.[107]

The kindly viewpoint adopted by Rudolf Steiner for that person, does not correspond to the full reality of the window with its three parts. For Zarathustra would not be portrayed in the left panel as having to struggle before finally being successful – as depicted in the right panel. A struggle in which he has to go through the tormenting crisis of overcoming earthly, ego-centric passions. For Zarathustra was already a very high initiate when he became the cultural leader of the primal Persian epoch, which started about 5,000 BC, and long before he enters the stage of world history in the sixth century BC. (One could perhaps suggest that the left panel shows a different person to those in the middle and right side panels; but this would be a structure contrary to all the other windows).

---

[105] Reported by S. Prokofieff, *Der esoterische Weg durch die 19 Klassenstunden*, p.108, quoting *Daniel J. van Bemmelen. Wiedergeboren am Beginndes Lichtalters*, by F. Lutters.

[106] The person reporting these words is using a very complex German expression (a 'Konjunktiv 1' mood) which, in a very precise usage can express some doubt as to exactly what was said by Steiner.

[107] See the *Two Gems from Rudolf Steiner*, lectures from 1904 & 1905.

GLOSSARY of some central anthroposophical terms

aeon: a long evolutionary time. There are seven of these, and we are now in the fourth such epoch. They are the called the Saturn, Sun, Moon, Earth (which has two halves, Mars & Mercury) Jupiter, Venus and Vulcan aeons.

Ahriman: an evil entity responsible for the attitude which sees matter as the only thing in creation, denying spiritual reality. He correlates to the Biblical term, Satan.

Angels: spiritual beings who are one aeon ahead of human beings in their evolution.

anthroposophy: a Greek word that literally means 'human soul wisdom'. In Rudolf Steiner's usage it means the wisdom that can dawn in a person's consciousness in their spiritual-soul; and which fully manifests when the Spirit-self is developed.

archangels: spiritual beings who are two aeons ahead of human beings in the evolution.

astral body: the soul, seen as an aura around the body.

astral realm: the Soul-world or soul realms, above the ethers, but below the Devachanic realms.

astrality: soul energies, but often it refers mainly to the feelings.

Cosmic Christ: the highest of the 'Powers' or sun-gods.

Devachan: the true heavens above the Soul-world; a Theosophical term from the Sanskrit meaning 'realm of the shining gods'. It is the realm of the archetypal Idea, of Plato.

the Double: a term usually referring to the Lower Self.

ego or self or I: the sense of self, but the eternal self is linked to this. Hence the ego is a dual or twofold thing.

egoism or egoistic: not quite the same as the well-known term egotism (which means conceit). Egoism is used by Rudolf Steiner to mean either the state of having a normal earth-centred ego, or that this earthly sense of self behaving in a selfish way.

etheric body: is made of the four ethers and duplicates the physical body's appearance. From it organic matter, such as new cells, are condensed.

ethers: subtle energies which sustain all living things on the Earth. Electricity and magnetism are formed as they decompose.

Group-soul: a spirit-being to whom all the animals of a particular species belong.

intellectual-soul: the rational, logical capacity.

intuitive-soul (see spiritual-soul)

Imagination, Inspiration, Intuition: Latin words for the three types of clairvoyance, which mean something different in everyday usage in English to the meanings that Rudolf Steiner gives them.

Imagination: the first stage of clairvoyance: this can be called 'psychic-image consciousness' for this results in astral or etheric images being perceived, (in normal English it usually means 'fantasy'.)

Imaginations: astral thought-forms.

Inspiration: this can be called 'cosmic-spiritual consciousness', perceiving or 'breathing-in' wisdom, from lower Devachan. (In normal English usually means a strongly felt creative urge or idea.)

Intuition: this can be called a 'high initiation consciousness'. It is a perceiving of, and inwardly becoming one with, another being. This state allows the seer to perceive at an upper Devachan level. (In normal English this usually means a semi-psychic awareness of something.)

intuition: can be used by Rudolf Steiner for the above high seership, but can sometimes appear in English anthroposophical texts in its usual English meaning of 'insights' (translating such German words as 'ahnen').

life-force: an alternative term for ether.

life-force organism: the ether body.

Life-spirit: the divinized etheric body, is made of Devachanic energies.

lower-self: the soul qualities that are tainted with Luciferic or Ahrimanic influences. It can be thought of as threefold, the lower thinking, feeling and will. But Rudolf Steiner also described it as sevenfold, being the lower qualities of the seven classical planets in astrology.

Lucifer: a 'fallen' entity who opposes the intentions of the higher gods, creating an ungrounded naïve attitude, but also instils a sense of self and enthusiasm for beauty, art and sensuality.

sentient-soul: the feelings, emotion (aspect of) the soul.

soul: appears as an aura, and contains the sentient-soul, intellectual-soul & spiritual-soul.

Spirit-human: the divine forces underlying the physical body, present in our subconscious will.

Spirit-self: the result of the purified and enlightened threefold soul-body or astral body.

spiritual-soul: also translated as 'consciousness soul', and could be called the intuitive soul. This is the soul capacity which underlies intuitive decision-making or intuitive flashes of insight. But it is also the most individualized or 'ego-ic' soul capacity, and can tend towards a hardened self-centredness.

spiritual-sun: the sun on its soul (or astral) level, behind the physical globe, and also on its actual spiritual level (also referred to as the Devachanic level): these levels comprise many energies and divine beings.

thinking: can be used to mean the exercise of our intelligence, but it is also used to mean any of the three clairvoyant states.

INDEX

Other publications on the Goetheanum windows:

Goetheanum Glasfenster	-	Georg Hartmann, Vlg. am Goetheanum, 1971
The Imagery of the Goetheanum Windows	-	Wilhelm Rath, Rudolf Steiner Press, 1976
Die Glasfenster-Motive des Goetheanum	-	Michaela Glöckler, undated, ca. 2013
Goetheanum Glasfenster	-	Albert Schmelzer, Vlg. am Goetheanum, 2013

Illustrations acknowledgements

1: In the Public Domain.
2: The author.
4: The author, based on the red window.
5A: Karlstejn: Wikimedia Commons (*Meister Theoderich*: geocities.com/Soho/Museum).
5B: From R. Knorr, in *Germania*: Korrespondenzblatt der Römisch-Germanischen Kommission des Deutschen Archäologischen Instituts Jahr V, 1921.
3, 6,7,11,13,14,15,17,21: Rudolf Steiner graphics, now in the Public Domain, courtesy of the Rudolf Steiner Nachlaßverwaltung, Dornach.
8: Above left: A Roman gold & heliotrope magical pendant, from ca. 300AD: Photo © **copyright Christies/ Bridgeman Images**. (The use of this image here does not in any way imply that the copyright holder shares the views about this image expressed in this book.)
Below left: From *Shared Shelf* database ID GL_19_075; courtesy, Antiquities library, Cornell Univ.
9: Public Domain: Franz Cumont, *Mysteries of Mithra*, Vol. 1, KPT, London, 1903.
10: Mithraic deities: Public Domain; Franz Cumont, *Mysteries of Mithra*, vol. 2, KPT, London, 1903.
12: Steiner Archive sketches: Public Domain, courtesy of Rudolf Steiner Nachlaßverwaltung.
16: Left: Courtesy of Cleveland Museum, USA.
Right: Wikimedia Commons.
18: Above left: Photo of Mithraic Statue, **copyright to Robert H. Consoli**, "Squinchpix.com" 2011.
Above right: Wikimedia Commons.
Mosaic of Orpheus and his lyre: Wikimedia Commons.
19: Above left: Courtesy J. Paul Getty Museum; in the *Open Content program.*
Above right: photo copyright to Marie-Lan Hguyen, 2006 (Wikimedia Commons).
Below: Gundestrup Cauldron: Wikimedia Commons.
20: Public Domain, courtesy of the Rudolf Steiner Nachlaßverwaltung.
22: The author.

Also by this author:

Living a Spiritual Year: seasonal festivals in both hemispheres (1992, new edition 2016)

The Way to the Sacred (2003)

The Foundation Stone Meditation: a new commentary (2005)

Dramatic Anthroposophy: Identification and contextualization of primary features of Rudolf Steiner's anthroposophy. (Ph.D. thesis, Otago University, 2005)

Two Gems from Rudolf Steiner (2014)

The Hellenistic Mysteries & Christianity (2014)

Rudolf Steiner Handbook (2014)

Horoscope Handbook – a Rudolf Steiner Approach (2015)

The Lost Zodiac of Rudolf Steiner - Exploring the four sets of zodiac images designed by Rudolf Steiner (2016)

See also Damien Pryor:

The nature & origin of the Tropical Zodiac
Stonehenge
The Externsteine
Lalibela
The Great Pyramid & the Sphinx

website: www.rudolfsteinerstudies.com

www.ingramcontent.com/pod-product-compliance
Lightning Source LLC
Chambersburg PA
CBHW061409090426
42740CB00026B/3490

* 9 7 8 0 9 9 4 1 6 0 2 3 2 *